WEALTH KRYPTONITE

KRYPTONITE

DISCOVER YOUR AVATAR AND SUPERPOWERS OF THE NEW RICH

WEALTH KRYPTONITE

DISCOVER YOUR AVATAR AND SUPERPOWERS OF THE NEW RICH

BY DAVID MILLER, CFP® AND RIDGELY GOLDSBOROUGH, ESQ.

ISBN: 978-0-692-83070-3

Library of Congress Control Number: 2017942574

Printed in the United States of America.

CONTENTS

DEDICATION

This book is dedicated to Kathy and Suzanne, the fabulous, powerful women that stand behind us and make us strong.

We also acknowledge our children who teach us on a daily basis as well as all global seekers who maintain a constant quest for self-improvement and self-awareness.

Lastly, we pay utmost respect to our team without whom none of our work would be possible. We are deeply grateful for their unending commitment to excellence in all areas and the example they set on a daily basis.

PREFACE

At some point in your life you will likely meet very smart people of seemingly substantial means who appear to be wealthy and yet in actuality, are not. Conversely, you may meet people of more modest means who despite the odds have created financial security and even amassed wealth.

Many books seek to explain that these different outcomes stem from a specific system or method. We take issue with that and do not agree with pigeon-holing anyone into a specific approach or set of behaviors that in turn dictates their success or lack thereof. After helping thousands of people achieve financial affluence over the last decade, we believe that the key to success lies not in a given system but rather in managing your emotions just as much, if not more than managing your money.

After years of interactions with all sorts of people, we have identified seven distinct profiles that define and clarify the behaviors and tenets of virtually any human being--particularly when it comes to money. We call these "Avatars" and those who understand both their own strengths and weaknesses (which we call Superpowers and Kryptonites) can use them to their distinct advantage.

When you understand the Avatars and can incorporate our three pillar approach of blending emotional, financial and tax intelligence, you move from being an Average Avatar to a Wealthy Avatar–someone who fits into the top 3% of all individuals in terms of financial means. It is a process and as with all things, requires a commitment. Along the way you will learn about other Avatars besides yours, how you interact with each of them as well their distinct relationship to loved ones and money. You will experience how your most important relations with family and colleagues (your Avatar Ecosystem) are affected on a moment to moment basis based on their Avatars. You will gain a deeper understanding of your own motivations--WHY you do what you do–and increase your awareness of what options lie in front of you at each given point.

It is our hope that armed with new insights and information you will accelerate your journey to greater emotional intelligence and wealth and perhaps improve your personal relationships in the process. Let this book act as a guide that you refer to often and share with those you most care about.

Money flows constantly through established practices and proven fundamentals. The key to building a dam that harnesses it, holds it and makes it available for your future use and enjoyment lies in gaining a more complete understanding of yourself. May this work serve as an accelerator to that process.

Wishing you great success,

David and Ridgely

Chapter 1

WHO ARE YOU?
What's your AVATAR?

"Narrow areas of expertise can be very productive.
Develop your own profile. Develop your own niche."

~ Leigh Steinberg

Why do we suffer a mid-life crisis? Or an identity crisis? Or a money crisis?

Why do people in seemingly stable circumstances melt down for no apparent reason and squander away their savings?

Do adverse winds suddenly blow in with such force as to thrust your economic lifeboat into a perfect financial storm and suck you into a bottomless whirlpool?

Of course not. **The fall happens gradually, seldom perceived until too late, one small mistake at a time, one poor decision, one tiny step in the wrong direction.** Cumulatively, the effects compound, the debt mounts, the bank account shrinks, the portfolio becomes the new check book and the results prove disastrous. And then the questions flow: "Why me? How did this happen?"

Interestingly, no one makes a single move without a belief system.

You don't get up in the morning unless you believe that rising holds more promise than staying in bed.

You don't eat unless you believe the act will fill your belly and remove your hunger pangs.

You don't work unless you believe you will be rewarded for your efforts.

Nothing happens without a belief.

Likewise, we make financial decisions based on those beliefs about money–right, wrong and all in between. These beliefs take on the nature of wire filaments. In isolation, they hold limited weight. However, as they wrap around and around each other, the collective belief system strengthens and the thousands of intertwined belief filaments morph into a giant cable that governs every decision we make.

Our beliefs determine WHY we do what we do. We become the personification of our beliefs through our actions.

Webster's Dictionary defines "avatar" as follows:
- Embodiment.
- Bodily manifestation.
- Someone who represents a type of person, an idea or a quality.

Google offers this definition:
- A manifestation of a deity or released soul in bodily form on earth; an incarnate divine teacher.
- An incarnation, embodiment, or manifestation of a person or idea.
- An icon or figure representing a particular person.

In other words, you have an Avatar based on WHY you do what you do–an Avatar, that perfectly fits all of these descriptions.

Your Avatar becomes the embodiment of your belief system.

Your Avatar physically manifests continually through your thoughts, words and deeds.

Your Avatar represents a type of person AND a particular dominant quality that you possess.

It explains in full living color WHY you take every action you take.

And importantly, it determines your relationship with money.

So where does it come from?

Your primary and most basic instinct as a human being is survival. Your secondary driving desire is the need for love and companionship.

Your Avatar stems from both, at the most primitive level.

Remember your infancy? When you craved milk as an infant what did you do?

You screamed and someone brought you milk. On an emotional level, following that "successful" action, screaming equals survival.

You then woke up in the middle of the night scared and alone. What did you do? You screamed again and someone came to comfort you. Now, screaming equals love and companionship.

From that point forward, any time you had a need or a want, you screamed. If it worked before, it will work again—until it didn't.

At such time as your caretakers stopped responding to your cries, your needs and wants nonetheless continued. If crying no longer got a response, you had to try something different, a new behavior or course of action.

When you found one that worked, you repeated it. And then you repeated it again. Like pieces of code wired into your personal programming, each successful act left and continues to leave a mental imprint.

That worked—do it again. This didn't—go back to plan A.

In short order your coding takes hold, like a computer program in the depths of your being. That proven pattern of behavior becomes your driver, how you survive and succeed in life.

It shapes, molds and forges your Avatar, WHY you think the way you think, WHY you speak the way you speak, WHY you do everything that you do.

Your Avatar quite literally takes over running your show. It is the engine that drives your decision-making based on early programming that met your most fundamental needs of survival and love.

The same patterns that govern your life, govern your relationship with money–whether you know them or not. Like the law of gravity, your Avatar affects every financial choice you make—whether you understand it, agree with it, or have any knowledge of it at all. Day by day, one decision after another, it takes complete command.

When you understand and embrace your Avatar, your financial landscape becomes more clear. Your motivations make more sense and flow seamlessly and elegantly. You gain immense clarity about who you are and how you view and operate in the world with respect to money.

It empowers and guides you.

When you live it, you acquire immense power—the power to take charge of your financial future and make it exactly what you want.

You answer the question: "WHO are YOU and how do YOU relate to money?"

The answer to that question will set you financially free.

Through your Avatar, you have unique strengths–like a Superhero with Superpowers.

Each Avatar also has its own unrivaled Kryptonite—a flaw or weakness to which that Avatar is susceptible.

In each case the Kryptonite is directly related to the Superpower, like its inverse quality, the perfect antithesis to the Superpower's greatest strength.

When you fully understand both, you can maximize your power and neutralize the Kryptonite. You bring forth your full potential, your talent, and your gifts. You can chart your path to financial independence with clarity.

When you understand your own Avatar and how to use it, you recognize and appreciate the Avatars of others and will temporarily discard your own Superhero cape in favor of another to accomplish a goal—with the understanding that you will naturally default back into your own identity with ease. This gives you great power, the ability to collaborate and cooperate with others, flexibility and understanding with loved ones–which as we will explore, is critical to building a solid economic base.

Let's take a look at the
seven Avatars.

Which do you resonate with the most?

GIVER

CONNECTOR

PROBLEM SOLVER

INNOVATOR

PERFECTIONIST

REBEL

MASTER

Avatar #1:

GIVER

"We make a living by what we get,
but we make a life by what we give."

~ Winston Churchill

Suppose that as an only child, you receive praise when you help and support your parents. Or suppose that as the youngest sibling, you do favors for your brothers and sisters to gain favor or avoid angst.

Whatever your station, to survive you naturally repeat the behavior of giving until it becomes a pattern. When you help or support, you survive and thrive.

Naturally and without conscious thought, this becomes the way you live. It never changes.

When you share yourself with those around you and contribute, life shines on you. When you don't, you feel empty, uncertain, confused, without a rudder or compass to guide you.

With this Avatar as your driver, you live to give to others, to add value to their lives, to have an impact with your actions and efforts.

You enjoy being part of a greater cause, participating in it and offering your service.

In your relationship with money, your Avatar exhibits much generosity. You enjoy picking up the tab, giving gifts and inviting others to join you in most any endeavor, often on your dime. As a Giver, for you money flows freely. You enjoy sharing it with others and making a difference in their lives, in all ways, large and small.

PRO AND CON

- The Giver wants to make a difference and contribute however and wherever possible.
- The Giver also has great difficulty saying no and therefore over fills their plate, often causing stress and angst both personally and professionally.

Avatar #2:

CONNECTOR

"Trust is the glue of life. It's the most essential
ingredient in effective communication. It's the
foundational principle that holds all relationships."
~ Stephen Covey

Imagine that early on, you endure a string of broken promises. A person in a position of authority fails to come through, tells you shady stories or lies to you.

Perhaps they violate your trust to even greater degrees.

You vow internally not to behave that way, never to treat others the way you have been treated. You tell yourself that you will act in the exact opposite fashion.

You WILL be counted on, reliable, dependable. Trust turns into your true North, the only way you can live. It guides every decision you make.

With this Avatar as your driver, you strive to build relationships based in trust.

You believe that trust is paramount and will work hard to create it in all aspects of your life.

When it comes to money, your Avatar acts cautiously. You generally pay your bills on time or even early, as a manifestation of your trustworthiness. You appreciate a good deal, though would seldom stiff someone or shirk your obligations—especially if you have made a commitment in some way. As a Connector, your word is your bond and of course this translates to your finances.

PRO AND CON

- The Connector values bonds and relationships above all else and is loyal to a fault.
- The Connector also goes far beyond the norm to build trust often at the expense of themselves and their well-being.

Avatar #3:

PROBLEM SOLVER

"Entrepreneurs go through real problems and come up with real solutions. It's not fake. You can do all the right things and still lose. You can do all the wrong things and still win."
~ Ben Huh

You believe in making sense out of things, simplifying and clarifying wherever possible. The origins of this can be widespread–either stemming from a negative environment in which you needed to survive or simply because you figured out that your path to success comes from problem solving and uncovering solutions.

Perhaps as a child, you experience constant confusion—separated or single parents, stepparents that don't relate or pay attention, siblings that appear favored over you, a chaotic home life.

To survive, you must sort out the mess. Perhaps you become a quasi parent to younger brothers or sisters, protect them or serve as their custodian.

Maybe you have to take care of yourself because no one else does.

To stay alive and subsist, you have no choice but to take in your circumstances, figure them out and problem solve.

When you do, things work out. You carry on. You endure. You become really good at processes, better than those around you. You like puzzles and figuring things out–and you are quite adept at it.

Confronting challenges and sorting them out grows into your modus operandi. Like it or not, you can't help yourself. It's what you do.

With this Avatar as your driver, you carefully observe all that is around you, take in elements of every situation and make sense out of them.

With respect to money, you exhibit a knack for finding methods of making more when needed and sorting your way out of financial jams. As a Problem Solver you will always find a solution if you focus on the challenge. Another alternative will present itself when sought and provide another financial option for you.

PRO AND CON

- The Problem Solver has an uncanny ability to sort out challenges, offer options and provide excellent alternatives.
- At the same time, in the absence of sufficient data, the Problem Solver freezes like a deer in a headlight and cannot move forward.

Avatar #4:

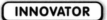

"My view is there's no bad time to innovate."
~ Jeff Bezos

You thrive on improving all that you touch. Seldom does anything cross your path that can't be adjusted, tweaked or altered in some way. The genesis of this drive can be either positive because you find excitement in any perceived potential for change, or negative because bettering things represented the only way you worked yourself out of difficult or painful circumstances in your youth.

Perhaps a disgruntled or dissatisfied father or another authority figure pushes you. You play sports and quickly determine that winning brings accolades.

For you, praise and reward come from successful competition, mostly over others, sometimes over yourself.

You learn that innovation and improvement surprise people much to your delight. You make it your driving force. Seldom is anything quite good enough.

You feel compelled to share your enhancements and advances with others who admire and compliment you for them.

You constantly seek better ways of doing virtually everything. Nothing else will ever satisfy you.

With this Avatar as your driver, you seek to improve most everything you touch. You want to tweak, make adjustments and innovate with a constant quest to find bigger, better or faster.

When it comes to money, new ideas and innovations lead to financial opportunities. An improvement to an existing system opens up new revenue streams. Novel approaches garner interest from others who will invest in you. Even when one idea fails to pan out, you seldom lose hope because another tweak to something else follows in its wake—and that, too, can be profited from.

(PRO AND CON)

- The Innovator thrives on making things better and improving virtually any process, system or approach they encounter.
- The Innovator also seeks to change things, often when unwarranted or unwanted.

Avatar #5:

PERFECTIONIST

"Fix your eyes on perfection and you make
almost everything speed towards it."
~ William Ellery Channing

In a rigid or strict environment, you quickly adapt. Follow the rules, stay alive. Break the rules, watch out.

Perhaps a strict disciplinarian instills a sense of order. Play within the guidelines, receive approval and admiration. Step over the line and suffer the consequences.

Alternatively, you find freedom inside clear parameters. You appreciate that boundaries actually create space for exploration in a safe environment.

You determine that systems and processes yield predictable results and that life works better when under control.

Mess occupies little space in your world. Disorder leads to problems. Stability comes from constancy and solidity.

Since there is a correct way to do things, why not do them that way?

With this Avatar as your driver, you believe there is a right way to do things and that things should be done right. You seek out effective systems, do not cut corners or skimp on the details.

When it comes to money, your Avatar knows that proven systems yield predictable results. You feel no need to re-invent the wheel. Rather, you look for established processes and solid track records in which to place your investments. As a Perfectionist, you like to track your results, watch over your resources carefully and pay close attention to your assets—with periodic reviews and good financial planning.

PRO AND CON

- The Perfectionist does things properly and finds systems that will create predictable results on which we can depend.
- The Perfectionist can also be quite stiff and rigid in their approach, often closed off to options proposed by others.

Avatar #6:

REBEL

"I don't worry. I don't doubt. I'm daring. I'm a rebel."
~ Mr. T

You don't fit in. Conventional feels wrong. Conforming goes against your gut. You don't belong in the pack—never have, never will.

Despite opposition, you rebel. Forced to kowtow, you cringe. The four walls of the box suffocate you. You must get outside.

Different is your normal. You don't understand or relate to standard protocol. While it may make you an outcast, you can't help it. When you challenge the status quo you feel most alive.

For you survival means pushing the envelope. Dare or despair.

With this Avatar as your driver, you live outside the box and rebel against the typical or classical way of doing things. Challenging the norm trumps conformity every time.

With respect to money, your Avatar doesn't change its modus ope-randi. You are unafraid of taking a risk, perhaps even comfortable with decisions that would be difficult for others who prefer the straight and narrow. As a Rebel, aggressive or alternate approaches appeal to you. Why follow mainstream wisdom when greatness lies in challenging it?

PRO AND CON

- The Rebel defies convention and takes all of us to new heights, through daring ideas and unique perspectives.
- The Rebel can also push others way with different and outside the box thinking that can lead to isolationism.

Avatar #7:

MASTER

"What the caterpillar calls the end of the world,
the master calls a butterfly."
~ Richard Bach

You grow up in an academic family. Your parents constantly study. Alternatively, perhaps they themselves lacked scholastic opportunities and push you relentlessly in their stead.

Knowledge equals power and rewards. Good grades reign supreme. Anything less equals failure.

Satisfaction comes from mastery, though true mastery eludes you—an unattainable goal though a perpetual quest.

Dive deep. Push all in. Prod, plunge, explore, seek the next level. Satisfaction lies in the infinite. You have an innate ability to hunt for more--more profundity, a new floor or outer boundary.

With this Avatar as your driver, you seek deep amounts of information over a broad variety of topics. You pick specific subjects and begin to learn about them, often for the sheer joy of curiosity and learning something new.

Even the study of money fascinates you. Your Avatar relishes learning more, going to the next level of understanding, grasping the intricacies of how it works. Your high level of intelligence makes you marketable and able to earn higher salaries and wages than most. As a Master, you appreciate others who recognize your talent and pay you for it.

PRO AND CON

- The Master's mind and knowledge range broad and far on a wide variety of topics that he or she will gladly share.
- The Master's intellect can at times prove so vast that it gets lost in complexity or intricacies that others cannot grasp.

Did you recognize yourself?

In all likelihood, you will have resonated with several of the Avatars, seen elements of yourself in more than one, related strongly to a few— as you should have.

As complex human beings we take on tendencies of others for myriad reasons. We seek to belong, to find ourselves, to gain clarity. We put on the capes of other Superheroes, sometimes out of desire, more often to survive.

Yet, at our core, in our essence, we find purity, a place from which we originate, a well that runs deep, a being-ness.

And, we make financial decisions from that essence, based on what we believe. Our Avatar drives our financial machine.

Did you identify your core Avatar?

Whether you did or did not, don't worry—we can help you do that and when you do, you'll find that discovering your Avatar is like coming home. A light bulb goes off. You get YOU—like being reintroduced to yourself or gaining an insight into the way you view the world for the first time, including your finances.

What a joy! For perhaps the first time, you gain access to your mental programming—the code that has run you for your entire existence.

When you flick a switch and the light comes on, the room looks different in an instant. A cave dark for ten thousand years brightens with a single candle. Discovering your Avatar feels just like that—a burst of instant clarity.

What if you have been making fundamental money mistakes for years? What if you could fix those moving forward? What if you can re-chart your financial future based on truly understanding your relationship with money?

We think, speak and act based on our Avatar.

It affects EVERYTHING, especially our decisions around money.

When you discover your Avatar, you take command. You determine your future based on your strengths, your superpower.

Of course, **it pays handsomely to be aware of your weakness, your Kryptonite.**

SUMMARY:

- No one does anything without a belief system.
- Your belief system manifests in physical form as your Avatar.
- Your Avatar guides and influences every decision you make and every action you take.
- You also have a unique strength, a Superpower and a corresponding weakness, a Kryptonite. It pays to know both.

CALL TO ACTION:

Read through the Avatar descriptions to recognize which might be yours. Trust your intuition. You are the most qualified person on earth to determine your own Avatar.

Chapter 2

KRYPTONITE – YOUR DEADLY ATTRACTION?

Do you act like a Superhero with financial Superpowers or does your Kryptonite turn you into an economic weakling?

"Sometimes people don't want to hear the truth
because they don't want their illusions destroyed."

~ Friedrich Nietzsche

Each Avatar has a Superpower, a driver that lies at the core of its belief system, a way in which that Avatar manifests itself on a continuous basis. Interestingly, each Avatar also has a Kryptonite, a weakness or challenge that can cripple the effectiveness of the Superpower if not properly managed and controlled.

The two battle each other constantly. The Kryptonite weakens the Avatar, looks to lure it away from manifesting its Superpower, acts as a distraction, a sidebar or a flat out blockage. Pay attention and you will discover that **the Kryptonite is akin to the opposite of the Superpower, inversely related, yet so close.**

It lurks in the shadows like a deadly attraction and without careful vigilance will bring ruin to even the most stalwart and dedicated.

Let's examine each Avatar in more detail and how the struggle unfolds between the Superpower and Kryptonite. Herein lies the difference between victory and defeat, happiness and misery and of course, wealth versus poverty.

Avatar #1: The Giver

"You will soon break the bow if you keep it always stretched."

~ Norman Vincent Peale

Although you yourself don't need to be the cause nor share the spotlight, you relish being part of a cause, participating in it and offering your service.

You love to support, and rejoice in the success of the overall plan, the company, the team, the family reunion, or whatever the cause may be.

Often you help behind the scenes, looking for ways to make the world a better place. Other times you may give in more of a public forum, trumpeting a movement or a message. You are a go-to person, the one people look for when they need help with just about anything.

 SUPERPOWER: Cause(s).

You become energized when you contribute to others, when you participate in a cause of any kind, large or small.

From helping an elderly person across the street to making coffee for your colleagues at the office to founding a charity to support the homeless or igniting a nation to eliminate oppression, you never stop giving—and it makes you feel great about YOU—at home, at the office, among friends, at your church, everywhere.

When you add value to others, your motor turns on and gets revved up.

When you make a difference for others, your tank fills and you feel complete and empowered.

When your actions have an impact, your personal capacity increases. Every time you give to a cause you gain even greater powers.

👀 KRYPTONITE: Over-commitment.

You are wired to say "yes" to most requests. For many Givers, saying no is actually painful and generally difficult. As a result, your plate fills up, sometimes to capacity and beyond. You become stretched too thin leading to stress or angst and occasionally mistakes happen as details fall through the cracks. You feel like your life belongs to others with so many requests flowing your way. You get bogged down in "little things" that take up time and energy. Over-commitment slows down your ability to contribute to other causes and can actually sabotage your desire to give to the greater good.

From a fiscal standpoint over-commitment can be the kiss of death. Nothing gets done properly because you are strained to capacity. You give so much that resources are stressed thin. In response to the many requests, capital gets disbursed too quickly, leaving none for a rainy day. You make yourself vulnerable to financial attacks.

People know that you seldom say "no" and make you the go-to person when they need anything, deserved or not. They know you will forgive quickly and take advantage. They will never stop as long as your Kryptonite remains in charge. It is a slippery, dangerous slope.

◈ SOLUTION: Get help.

Use advisors to determine what causes make sense and contribute to those. Find someone who can help you say "no" and act as a financial firewall between you and your assets. In other words, you can't make a "decision" without consulting them, a layer of insulation that will protect you.

We are who we are. For the Giver, avoiding your Kryptonite means building a support team. You will never stop giving. You need protection from yourself so you are able to learn and embrace the act of receiving.

KRYPTONITE STORY: Kids gone WILD!

A married couple in their late seventies, with a brokerage account of about $2,500,000 and a house paid off, came to the office in a distressed state. Beginning in 2002, Carol and Steve began to "loan" money to their grown sons to finance their new business. Every year since then, the "boys" continued to borrow, until the number topped a million dollars. At one point, Carol and Steve even took a line of credit on their own house to pay off the mortgages of their boys' homes.

In 2014, Steve had a quadruple heart bypass along with other major health problems. Now, Steve is back at work selling real estate to avoid using up the remainder of their personal savings–all because they could not say "no" to their children.

MORAL OF THE STORY:
If you can't say "no," get a trusted advisor who can.

Avatar #2: The Connector

"I wasted time and now doth time waste me."

~ William Shakespeare

To build connections, you strive to create relationships based in trust.

You become educated as an expert in a particular subject and work hard to demonstrate your expertise as a way of establishing trust.

Your friendships run deep and people know you as someone who has their back. You do things "right" in order to show that you are trustworthy and will go the extra mile to prove it with your actions, words and deeds.

Recognition matters and you work hard to instill pride, both for yourself and among those that surround you. You have great value and want others to be aware of that. You are reliable and can be counted on. If you say you are going to do something, you do it and those around you appreciate you.

SUPERPOWER: Trust

When you establish trust, everything is possible. Deep bonds create a foundation and a platform from which you soar. Connections with others come before anything and once established build the necessary bridge for progress. In a space of safety, your talent shines forth.

Respect gives you strength. With parameters that can be relied on, you open up your potential and play full out. When trust is cherished and nurtured, your power increases exponentially. When you Connect and build Trust you become empowered.

👀 KRYPTONITE: Waste

Connectors have such a strong drive to connect that they will go far beyond the norm to demonstrate their Superpower of Trust to others. You go the extra mile and then another extra mile and then another one for someone else—in the hopes of demonstrating your trustworthiness. While your first extra mile makes you "extraordinary", any effort beyond that just makes you nice. In other words, much of that extra effort become Waste. Through the extra, extra, extra effort, you end up wasting a lot of time and energy without accomplishing your objective of proving your trustworthiness. This leads to frustration and anxiety and a feeling of "why don't they get it?" about others who interpret your heroic efforts as niceties.

Financially, you often get stuck in the details and lose sight of the forest for the trees. The zest and zeal to prove your trustworthiness and pay everything on time, every time, can leave your coffers depleted with small unimportant things taken care of at the expense of the bigger challenges that can actually move your business needle. A rush to "check off the list" can prevent you from careful consideration and the need to noodle and ponder matters from multiple angles before making deliberate, well thought out decisions. It's the "stepping over a dollar to pick up a penny" syndrome. The covenant to "pay bills on time" takes center stage and in the world of business "cash" is largely still king.

◇ SOLUTION: Find trusted advisors with different viewpoints.

This is critical for the Connector. Identify the person with the ability to make "tough financial calls" and listen closely to their counsel. Make planning a priority and exercise sound financial judgment by adhering to the plan–not the noise in the marketplace or at the office. Find an accountability partner, either a paid professional or a trusted colleague to help you stick to your goals without getting stuck in the weeds. Set up periodic reviews of your numbers with your advisor so as to keep your head above water and focused on the long-term goals and objectives.

 **KRYPTONITE STORY: How low can you go?**
90 year old Miss Jane called her grand-daughter in a state of upset. She received a credit card statement in her name that she knew nothing about, with charges in other states that she had never even visited. The grand-daughter naturally assumed it was fraud and that the charges could be reversed. She told Miss Jane to send down the statement and asked her grandmother for the card number to call the credit card company to place an alert and put a halt to any further charges. In conversation with the credit card company, it seemed as though the charges came from an individual with the same last name as Miss Jane–and further, that the credit card had been maxed out to its limits. How strange. How could this be? As the mystery unfolded, it turns out that Miss Jane's own son, on a recent visit to attend a funeral in her town, had taken a credit card application from her desk, filled it out in Miss Jane's name, had the card sent to his own address in Florida and before anyone knew what happened, used the card for his own means–leaving Miss Jane holding the debt with virtually no recourse. She certainly wasn't going to prosecute her own offspring.

MORAL OF THE STORY:
Never tempt the hand of fate–shred unwanted applications and put your paperwork away.

Avatar #3: The Problem Solver

"Routine is not organization, anymore than paralysis is order."
~ Arthur Helps

You have an uncanny ability to observe what surrounds you and take in data. You process information, circumstances and input at warp speed—almost automatically, without conscious thought.

You take complicated, or what may appear to be complicated factors, problems and concepts and organize them to create options that are sensible and easy to implement.

You are highly "solution" oriented and typically can be viewed as an expert because you find alternatives quickly. In a brainstorming session, your colleagues know that they can count on you to provide multiple options.

You summarize complicated issues and break them down into easily digestible pieces to come up with answers. You are the person people look for when they want to work through something because you can clarify and simplify just about anything.

SUPERPOWER: Solutions

Solving life's puzzles energizes you. Coming up with answers to problems and issues fills you with satisfaction. Knowing that you can sort through things and offer solutions that work feeds your desire to help others.

Clarifying murky situations and shedding light on them brings you inner joy.

You relish the complex and thrive when required to rack your brain for resolutions. Simplifying processes and coming up with step-by-step procedures for success happens as a matter of course. When you make sense of anything, especially if complicated, your energy meter goes up. It invigorates you. When you solve problems and manifest Solutions you become empowered.

KRYPTONITE: Paralysis

When you can't see it or at least the path to the solution you get bogged down and grind to a halt. Paralysis grips you. You have a need for information, possibilities or perspectives and if you don't have those, you cannot formulate the needed solution. You get the "I'm here though not really present" look on your face and become bogged down. Your Superpower ceases to function and turns into confusion.

Unfortunately, your tendency in this moment is to withdraw and go into a shell or bury your head like an ostrich in the sand. This is the worst thing you could do inasmuch as the very answer to your paralysis lies outside of you. You need allies to provide options and alternatives or at least more data points to input into your highly capable processing brain. Your confusion and consternation must be replaced with lucidity and only when you gain clarity can you move forward again.

The financial implications of paralysis are obvious. You plainly don't act. While you don't make mistakes that way, neither do you make any progress.

SOLUTION: Build a network of trusted, logical thinking friends.

You need sensible and wise advisors for two reasons. First, when you find yourself paralyzed your advisors know what to do—get you more information and new takes on the issue at hand. Second, they can ensure that your problem-solving nature doesn't keep you putting Band-Aids on a sinking ship. In other words, sometimes you need to step back and ask the bigger question: "Even if I solve this problem, is that solution getting me any closer to my true goals and dreams?" Having a brain trust that you can tap into, especially of those who have walked the path before you, can make sure that short term fixes don't get in the way of the overarching objectives or plan.

KRYPTONITE STORY:
A Tale of Three Sisters

Miss Theresa finally tired of the cold winters in Delaware. At 83 she'd had enough. Her three daughters agreed that it was time for her to move South, so she put her house on the market and began to make plans. Tina, the oldest of the three really wanted her to move to Sarasota, Florida, a lovely town with many elderly, where Tina could take care of her. She took charge, figured out where Miss Theresa could live, shared the elderly community with her sisters and generally showed them why it made sense for Miss Theresa to reside near her. Mary Jo and Rebecca also offered though in the end, Tina won out and Miss Theresa packed up her things and got on a plane.

Tina, the problem solver, stepped in and took care of each challenge as it came up. She helped out with her mother's affairs, found a one bedroom house for her and generally looked after her banking. In fact, Miss Theresa set up all of her new accounts as joint accounts with Tina, to make everything easier with bill paying and such. Outside of the house, most of Miss Theresa's assets sat in her brokerage account.

A few years later, Miss Theresa passed away and left her estate in three equal parts to the three daughters. Except for one problem. The brokerage account, which was jointly titled with Tina, by operation of law became Tina's sole property upon Miss Theresa's death.

If not for Tina's sense of fairness, the only thing left to share would have been the small home.

MORAL OF THE STORY:
The devil, and the inheritance, is in the details. Pay attention!

Avatar #4—The Innovator

"Progress is impossible without change, and those who cannot change their minds cannot change anything."
George Bernard Shaw

Everything you touch, you want to improve. You flourish in making adjustments and tweaks to enhance whatever is in front of you. You question everything, wondering how it could be adapted or altered.

You can't stop yourself from looking at virtually anything to make it better and share your progress with the world.

You invent things and often associate from other disciplines or industries and apply what you learn to what you are working on. Tinkering, physically or with concepts, strategies and processes, comes naturally. You are a fountain of fresh ideas and innovative approaches.

SUPERPOWER: Improvements

Innovation excites you and brings out your best. When you upgrade a process or a system it fuels you. You thrive when you bring an enhancement to the team. You look at things and see a possible enrichment or a tweak that could make a huge difference.

You try things and keep only what complements and strengthens the process in front of you. You love new things, new ways, new approaches. When you Innovate and create Improvements you become empowered.

KRYPTONITE: Change (for change's sake)

Your Superpower drives you to seek improvements with everything and that very act can become your Kryptonite. Once you figure out the best way to make a morning coffee, the desire to make it better can actually make it worse. Proven processes often need no betterment and are best left alone.

The yearning for constant change can upset established procedures, cause negative disruption and lead to poor morale—or at best confusion or aggravation.

Other team members become disheartened or even annoyed when you, yet again, want to make another adjustment. To them it is disempowering and invalidating and creates a sense of "nothing is good enough." The obvious fall out from this is a loss of desire to set up processes and systems that work because the fear is that their efforts will not matter. You will want to change it anyway, so why bother. It also leads to a sense of "Oh, no, here comes the Innovator–what is he or she going to mess with this time?" This can result in poor productivity and a lack of teamwork. Change for change's sake alone does not serve.

Financially, constant change can prove disastrous. You think you know better so you sell out of one position and into another. And then you do it again even though it did not work so well the first time. Or you create and manufacture something for sale, only to decide that you can once again improve the prototype, rapidly driving up the development costs. Or you try a marketing campaign at a certain cost, only to want to change it before proper testing and baselines can be established. And so on. The need for reigning in the desire for change is paramount for the attainment of any level of long term success and wealth.

SOLUTION: Empower other team members and stay out of their way–including those who manage your finances.

This is easier said than done. You always want to influence and change everything and this desire is sincere as well as strong within you. You believe you can find a better way. The key to building a successful business is to put your talents to work where innovation is warranted and appreciated and to simply stay out of other areas, other departments, where proven systems and methodologies are in play. "You do your thing, let them do theirs" is a great motto for you. Obviously, this requires a trust level with your advisors and colleagues and the need to surround yourself with those that you can rely on enough to let go of their turf and focus on your own. When it comes to money, many skill sets are required and there is no way you can improve all of them.

KRYPTONITE STORY:
When the light bulb pops...

Our client's son, Freddy, always had "another bright idea." He attended a weekend real estate seminar titled "How to Make a Fortune in Real Estate without Investing a Dime of Your Own Money" and came away fired up and ready to roll. These self-appointed real estate gurus had a foolproof system. You borrowed money from credit card companies, used that money as the down payment for a fixer-upper, bought the house, quickly gave it a facelift and flipped it in time to pay back the credit card debt and leave yourself a nice profit. Then you had your credit lines intact to repeat the process. The gurus even provided applications from credit card companies who readily extended credit.

Freddy locked himself in his room in the basement of his parents' home where he still lived while he was getting his feet under him. He filled out every single application and sent them in without ever checking the credit interest rates. Why should that matter? He intended to pay them off in full. A bit surprisingly, seven different companies extended Freddy varying credit limits. It was time to go shopping. Not surprisingly, the real estate gurus also provided a list of available homes for sale in different price ranges. All Freddy had to do was choose the right one.

Without consulting us, our client agreed to co-sign on the loan–especially since Freddy was providing the entire down payment. All he needed was his parents' credit and they wanted to help their son get his business started. Freddy bought a house and began to work on it. With limited mechanical skills, the repairs took longer than expected and furthermore, Freddy was no speed demon with a paint brush. Three months later, with the house finally ready, he put it on the market. Although he received many credit card notices in the mail, he never opened a single one. Making a payment was never part of the plan.

Regrettably, the market conditions did not seem as advertised and the house did not budge. After two months and with no credit left on his cards, Freddy rented the house for what he could get, $700 per month less than the actual mortgage payment. Because Freddy had no income and no more credit, our client ended up paying the difference for almost two years. Freddy ended up with a house alright–completely under water along with a mountain of credit card debt.

At least our client didn't co-sign on the credit cards.

MORAL OF THE STORY:
If it seems too good to be true, run.

Avatar #5: The Perfectionist

"Success makes men rigid and they tend to exalt stability over all the other virtues; tired of the effort of willing they become fanatics about conservatism."
~ William Lippman

You believe there is a correct way to do things and that things should be done right. You seek out effective systems, do not cut corners or skimp on the details. You follow procedures and are results driven.

If the proper system is followed, you achieve accurate and predictable results, those desired by the company or enterprise. You create structures and practices for clarity and simplicity and the flawless running of operations. You take notes and pay attention to successful processes.

You are precise and deliberate and excellent at organizing. You create order and arrangements that work.

SUPERPOWER: Systems

When order prevails, you shine. When you implement standard operating procedures, results flow. When you bring into play a proven system, you light up. Effectiveness and competence drive you.

Correct measures lead to better results and you seek them out. When you find the right way to do anything, your batteries get an instant charge. Predictability leads to forecasting and forecasting is a way of looking into the future and preparing for it. You thrive on processes and procedures, all of which are set up by proper structures.

When you perfect anything and install a system to run it you become empowered.

👀 KRYPTONITE: Rigidity

At times, your drive to implement systems stifles the creativity of others. In addition, rigid systems that create rules take away others' ability to think for themselves and you may find yourself with many monkeys on your back. A common response to "too many rules" becomes "well, just tell me what to do and I'll do it." This immediately dumps work back on you as opposed to driving people to seek solutions on their own.

Rigidity can also cause colleagues to stagnate and not reach for alternatives or foster healthy conflict that leads to innovation. Too much marching to the drum beat can lead to automatons that show up, punch a clock and leave–with little feeling or genuine concern for the organization. Systems will always have their place in successful organizations. Rigidity simply slows everything and everyone down.

From a fiscal perspective, a lack of fluidity and flexibility means less options. While slow and steady does indeed win the race, at the same time, business moves faster than ever today and the ability to be nimble and adjust quickly can make or break a project. What worked yesterday can be obsolete today, pointing to the need for "business at the speed of thought" often an uncomfortable space for a Perfectionist.

◈ SOLUTION: Operate from a clear plan.

A plan in and of itself is a system and therefore this falls right into your bailiwick. You are a great operator and a proven leader of execution. The key is have others assist in the creation of the plan itself–including trusted advisors who have already developed processes that work. The second key is to have clear accountability to the plan and outside counsel that provide expansive perspectives and alternate approaches.

KRYPTONITE STORY: Connect the .dots!

In the late 90s a client came up with a brilliant idea. In the early days of assigning internet addresses, he had a contact with a broker in Australia who had an inside line on the dot.LA extension. Outside of the standard .COM, .NET, .ORG, and .GOV, most of the extensions referenced their country of origin, generally tied to their English spelling of the country's name. Therefore, .CA stood for Canada, .FR for France, .UK for the United Kingdom and so on. This Australian broker had a relationship with a senior official in the government of Laos and assured our client that he could get him as many domains of the .LA extension as he wanted, for a small fee of $450,000.

Our client went nuts, dreaming of all of the .LA domains that would translate into millions of dollars in revenue in both Los Angeles and Louisiana. Imagine movies.LA, hotels.LA, cars.LA, stars.LA, rent.LA, beach.LA and so on in Southern California and sausage.LA, music.LA, cajun.LA, gators.LA and so on in Louisiana. He came up with a list of almost 5,000 .LA domains and sent it to Australia.

Despite our concerns and candid advice on the need for proper documentation, government assurances, a more detailed paper trail and references on the broker, the client would not listen. With dollar signs in his eyes, he wired almost half a million dollars to a bank in Australia and for a brief while, it looked as though all would pan out brilliantly. The client began to build an online platform to broker these domains.

Then, overnight, the government changed in Laos and simply appropriated all of our client's domains. Out went the old guard, in came the new and our client quickly found out that the United States government will do little for an individual in a foreign land, particularly in a third world country. With little to show in the way of documents, the client kissed that money goodbye.

MORAL OF THE STORY:
When it comes to business transactions, be sure to "dot" your "i"s.

Avatar #6: The Rebel

"Isolation is the sum total of wretchedness to a man."
~ Thomas Carlyle

You live outside the box and rebel against the typical or classical way of doing things. You challenge the status quo and seek unique approaches that no one else has considered to existing problems and challenges.

Nothing stunning happens inside the square—no greatness, nor anything exciting. If the average person goes right, you choose left or question whether you need to move at all.

You are often entrepreneurial and love disruption, particularly if it is a "game changer". You think differently than others and look to create a market versus serve one. You have a broad variety of diverse interests in food, music, art and friends and can be sometimes seen as different, intriguing and unique. How exciting!

SUPERPOWER: Challenge

You come alive outside the mold, away from the norm. You pursue alternatives, those that others don't focus on or even see–and this unique approach creates new and innovative solutions that may even be disruptive. You gravitate to the offbeat and appreciate divergence. The outlandish or peculiar seems familiar.

You never conform to the traditional, finding no comfort there. You separate from the middle of the road, the vanilla, the bland. Convention bothers you and seems pointless. When you rebel against the norm and challenge the status quo you become empowered.

KRYPTONITE: Isolation

Your need to challenge most everything can put you at odds with others. They may feel as if you constantly take issue with them or their work. It causes them to push you away or shy away from you because you make them nervous with your outlandish ideas. Most people are afraid or at least uncomfortable with change whereas you relish it.

When you think outside the box and proffer unusual approaches, others may shun them as non-traditional and risky. You will often find yourself without much support for some of the ideas that you put forth. Others feel attacked or threatened by your eccentric take and do not have the same comfort zone at all. Frequently, they will push you away and you may feel equally desirous of distancing yourself from them. This causes isolation and the creation of silos. If not careful, you may find yourself on an island, alone with your unique and different ideas.

When it comes to money, you will have challenges finding allies because conformity, compromise and even collaboration go against your very nature.

You first have to sell your idea as revolutionary or disruptive or immensely novel–and then you have the further difficulty of getting investors to trust that you, the Rebel, are the right person to execute it. Money follows rules and likes systems, the very concepts that you rebel against. Further, it is challenging to accomplish anything remarkable in the absence of a team and building one, for you, may not prove easy.

SOLUTION: Make others aware of your Avatar AND with that awareness select a limited number of close advisors.

Think about it. Most people don't like to have their views and ideas challenged. Your nature is to challenge them. If, on the other hand, a colleague knew ahead of time that you are a Rebel, they would expect you to challenge everything. You morph from being contrarian to unique, different and always able to offer an outside-the-box approach– in other words, you become "cool". You want a few close advisors who understand your nature and will not hesitate to point out the downside of "rebelling" in any particular situation. They can act as filters for you, the "voice of reason" and while you won't always choose to follow their advice, you certainly want to listen to their perspective.

KRYPTONITE STORY:
Me and My Red Corvette!

A husband and wife team each had IRA accounts that we managed. In 1999, certain investors feared a potential Y2K meltdown of the marketplace that led to a fair amount of panic, especially regarding software challenges. The fear stemmed from the fact that the computer experts realized that most software was written with the last 2 digits representing the year as opposed to all four digits, making 2000 indistinguishable from 1900. The wife followed and fully embraced this line of reasoning. She deduced that the markets would all crash and she would lose her retirement account. Based on this conclusion she felt that the best thing to do would be to buy a new sports car–either a Firebird or a Corvette. Her husband called us in a panic himself indicating she wouldn't listen to him and that we needed to talk to her. We spoke with her more than once to reassure her that there was no need to panic about Y2K and explained the penalties and income tax she would incur if she prematurely invaded her IRA. Our dialogue had no impact, as she withdrew all the funds in her IRA and bought a new sports car!

MORAL OF THE STORY:
Sometimes Momma just needs a new ride.

Avatar #7: The Master

"Dealing with complexity is an inefficient and unnecessary
waste of time, attention and mental energy.
There is never any justification for things being complex
when they could be simple."
~ Edward de Bono

With this Avatar as your driver, you seek deep amounts of information over a broad variety of topics. You pick specific subjects to learn about, often for the genuine joy of curiosity and ingesting something new. Interestingly, the sheer journey of learning is often enough to pique your interest. You don't even need a specific motivation such as job research or career growth. Sometimes learning for the sake of learning is joy enough for you–whatever the subject matter.

You gather and retain substantial knowledge in different areas and can typically be viewed as an "expert" in numerous disciplines by many, though you may insist that you have yet to truly master any of them. Since the power is in the learning, mastery, while interesting, is elusive and therefore not something that you want to lay claim to. Still, you are fearless about new subjects or ideas and unafraid to delve into a topic regardless of previous history with it. For you the very act of absorbing and exploring anything novel is in itself noble and worthy.

🌟 SUPERPOWER: Depth

Deep thinking causes your creative juices to bubble forth. You relish intellectual stimulation and a healthy debate–especially when spiced up with data, facts, figures and unique perspectives. The ability to sit down and dissect a point or a proposition to significant extents excites you. Why not go all the way to the bottom with it?

The presence of high levels of intelligence vitalizes you. Profound study and analysis feed your genius and help it grow. Whether at three o'clock in the morning in an obscure online forum or at a think tank weekend with other brainiacs, you will latch onto any opportunity to expand your mind. Mastery of subjects gives you quiet confidence, across a broad array of subjects.

Exploration and investigation excite you.

What makes the perfect Manhattan? Is it the way you squeeze the Maraschino? One ice cube versus two? The blend of bourbon? The temperature? The combination of several elements? The very study of it all? When you master things and seek out depth you become empowered.

😵 KRYPTONITE: Complexity

The drive for depth and an understanding of the innate intricacies in a project can often lead to unwanted complexity. Others may not care about the machinations of how a particular tool works—all they care about is the product or the result. Most people don't concern themselves over how Wi-Fi signals travel from the farthest corner of the earth and convert into sound files that through a mobile interpreter emerge as a live voice in their headset. They just need to know what button to push to talk to Mom.

When you add unnecessary or unwanted complexity, you isolate others who either don't understand or don't concern themselves about the inner workings.

They do not share the fascination for "how" things work, down to the intricate details. Moreover, because much of what you know, as a Master, is out of the mental league of the rest of us, it's annoying and even patronizing to listen to. No one wants to feel mentally unworthy.

In addition, complexity often leads to increased cost, an unwanted by-product, in two areas. It adds time which costs money. And it adds steps, components, pieces, elements–that require greater physical costs.

Financially speaking, mastery seldom translates directly to wealth. The love of study–of the markets, the trends, the data–can overshadow the need to make a clear, clean plan and execute it over a prolonged period. The quest for more depth can overshadow the basics. Money is not complicated. To accumulate it, we need an unburdened plan with a straight path ahead of it. Too much depth can make it unwieldy, awkward and clumsy and too many twists and turns often cause you to miss the actual road.

◈SOLUTION: Select highly intelligent, yet firm financial advisors.

If they are not well studied, well-versed and of a significant intellect, you will have a hard time heeding their counsel. At the same time, left to your own devices you will create a fiscal plan that is too convoluted or complex and cumbersome to manage–which generally means that it will be abandoned before it can bear fruit. Find advisors who can go toe-to-toe with your finely honed mind, yet bring you down to earth when it comes to the basic money fundamentals. This is not a journey that you want to go alone.

KRYPTONITE STORY:
What's Up DOC?

A physician ran a highly successful specialty practice making mid to high six figures. When approached with an opportunity to partner with a Physicians Assistant (PA) to found a medical clinic where the PA would be the primary practitioner, he jumped on it. As the practice initially succeeded, the physician became lazy with the day to day activities of the clinic and spent the majority of his time at his specialty practice. The office manager ran every aspect of the clinic with no oversight from the physician. To complicate matters, the office manager of the clinic was married to the PA.

When the physician needed to open a line of credit for the clinic, he asked our firm to complete the tax returns that had not been filed for the prior two years. As we began to pull the financial data together to compile the financial statements, we requested bank statements, credit card statements, new loans and loan balances. Our request to the office manager was met with resistance and refusal. After weeks of requests, we finally involved the physician. As we received the requested documents and performed our analysis, we observed that the bank statements had credit card payments and loan payments with no documentation. We quickly realized that something was not kosher.

At this point, a reasonable person would insert themselves to ensure we got to the bottom this problem. Unbelievably, the physician did nothing. After months of requesting information, with opposition at every step of the way, we prepared to disengage the client. It all came to a head when the physician skipped his own personal payroll check due to a lack of cash in the business bank account. Finally, with his full attention and help, we concluded that the office manager had opened multiple credit cards in the name of the business and racked up nearly $85,000 of personal charges. The business itself borrowed $275,000 from a local bank and those funds were used to remodel the home of the office manager and the PA. As if this was not bad enough, the physician could not fire either of them. In an act of laziness, the physician never reviewed the operating agreement of the clinic. While the parties had equal ownership, the PA had complete operating control of the clinic.

MORAL OF THE STORY:
High earning ability or a brilliant mind, does not necessarily correlate to business and money management.

VERY IMPORTANT NOTE:

Even though every one of us has our own Avatar that guides us and influences us, you will likely see a lot of yourself in others. Perhaps you feel like a blend of several Avatars. In actuality, you can don the cape of any other Superhero at any time if you understand it. In fact, this can strengthen and broaden your own capabilities and strengths whenever you need them.

You will however, always default back to that which is your essence, the Superpower of your Avatar. In other words, you have a base of power that is uniquely yours and will never change. How you use it and what other capes you choose to put on in any given moment is entirely up to you and will vary immensely from one person to another. In fact, this becomes the distinguishing factor that makes YOU uniquely YOU!

> "All interesting heroes have an Achilles Heel."
> ~ Jo Nesbo

SUMMARY:

- Your Avatar converts you into a Superhero with Superpowers.
- Every Superhero has a fatal flaw, a Kryptonite.
- When you master both, you can maximize your Superpower and minimize your Kryptonite.

CALL TO ACTION:

Recognize your Avatar fully and begin to understand it, particularly as it relates to money. Do you regularly use your Superpower? Can you relate to your Kryptonite or at least appreciate its presence in your life? Can you identify instances where it has affected you?

Chapter 3

YOUR AVATAR AND THE MONEY FLOW

"Business ideas are like those flying dragons in Avatar. First you have to find one, let it choose you, then be brave enough to ride it."

~ Ryan Lilly

Take a moment to ask those around you: "What is money?"
You will likely hear a broad range of answers:

The very question evokes all sorts of emotions and responses.
Consider this one: "Money is a form of energy."

Think about it. Most of the time we don't even see it. It transfers all around us from one person to another, one account to another, one entity to another.

Imagine that you are about to buy a house. Does it ever occur to you to go to the bank and say to the manager: "Excuse me, you are about to lend me half a million dollars. I'd like to make sure that you have it. Show me the money!"

Of course not. You assume it's there. You then sign a bunch of papers and allegedly, transfers happen from the bank to the seller, to the real estate agent, to the court for recording costs and so on to complete the transaction.

Here's the rub: No one ever sees the money.

It simply flows through the ethers from one place to another...just like energy.

And it continues to flow. Look around as you drive. You see an old pickup truck on your left and a new BMW sedan on your right. It takes less energy to acquire the truck than the sedan.

The energy of money flows constantly.

The big question becomes: Where are YOU in the flow?

To "stay in the flow", we need to understand the Four Laws of Prosperity and how each Avatar interacts with them. Here they are:

1. **The Law of Receiving.**
2. **The Law of Earning.**
3. **The Law of Spending.**
4. **The Law of Investing.**

#1: The Law of Receiving

"The deepest experience of the creator is feminine,
for it is the experience of receiving and bearing."

~ Rainer Maria Rilke

Before you are born, you cannot have a bank account. No one can open one for you. Stop by the bank and try it. Ask the teller to open a savings account for your unborn child. What will happen?

They can't do it.

So what is your first contact with money?

Someone gives it to you–an uncle, grandparent or parent.

Someone makes a gift and your first act with money is RECEIVING.

And yet, society, family members and even our peers often fill our brains with concepts and stories that run counter to our own openness when it comes to receiving money. They have ideas, passed down through generations that run like ticker-tapes in our brains.

Perhaps the most common notion is:

"It's better to give than receive."

Really? How can that be true?

Doesn't someone, by definition need to receive if someone else is giving? How can that automatically mean that "giving" is better than "receiving"?

Is the "giver" always better than the "receiver"?

Aren't both needed in any transfer? Why is one better than the other? Isn't "receiving" a necessary component of "giving"?

Fill in the following blank: "Rich people are _____."

What are the words that typically follow?

"Selfish. Greedy. Mean. Egotistical. Stingy. Self-centered." And so on.

The association that happens on an unconscious level is: "Since I don't want to be selfish, greedy or mean, then I definitely don't want to become rich."

This mental programming needs to be carefully examined and reconsidered. We need a new picture with respect to money.

If you walk by a marina and observe a group of well-to-do individuals enjoying an afternoon on a yacht, are they all selfish, greedy and mean? Of course not. Are there not many individuals with modest means who are also selfish, greedy and mean? Of course there are.

In other words, it has nothing to do with the money itself. Money is neutral. It has everything to do with each individual and their belief systems. However, if you hold a negative association with money and wealth, you will have a challenge with receiving.

Giving is good. Receiving is good.

Being open to RECEIVING is a necessary component of the flow of money. Any thought that blocks our ability to receive must be explored, dissected and rejected in order for us to achieve prosperity.

Interestingly, Givers, who are so used to contributing, seldom think of themselves. Therefore, receiving may seem foreign to them and this can hinder the money flow.

The rigidity of a Perfectionist can act as an inhibitor when the flow shows up in unfamiliar or non-systematic ways.

Conversely, the Rebel will challenge everything--including the tried and true methods of receiving and garnering wealth.

All Avatars must check in with their own long-held views on receiving. While most of us have been taught the value of "giving", receiving has often taken a back seat or even been condemned in our formative years and this programming must be questioned, shed light on and discarded in order to open the flow and keep it open.

#2: The Law of Earning

**"Your greatest asset is your earning ability.
Your greatest resource is your time."**

~ Brian Tracy

The free market does not reward desire, drive or best intentions. The market focuses only on results and the interchange of energy in the form of money.

You use your energy to provide a service. The marketplace pays you back with energy in the form of money.

You use your energy to produce a product. The marketplace buys it from you with energy in the form of money.

All of us have a basic hierarchy of needs, the primary of which are food, clothing and shelter. Until these are met, we focus exclusively on achieving them. The fact that you are reading this material right now means you have enough energy in your life to meet these basic needs. Otherwise, you would be hunting for food, making your clothes or building a shelter. In other words, you have extra energy for other things.

There are many things you can do with your energy at any given moment. You could go visit your family. You could go jogging. You might choose some other exercise to take care of your body. You might make a fabulous dinner for loved ones. Maybe you decide to take a stroll in a park.

All of these activities take energy. You can use your given amount of energy each day in many ways.

However, only when you put your energy to work in the free market will the market return energy to you as part of the flow. This is called EARNING (Law #2). You put your energy to work in the free market and the free market gives you energy in return in the form of money.

At that moment, you must RECEIVE (Law #1) that energy. Notice that the two laws work together.

The Law of EARNING by definition includes the Law of RECEIVING.

Certain Avatars may view this approach to earning as boring as it is so straightforward. The Innovator will seek better ways than the norm. The Rebel will challenge it. The Master finds it plebeian and uninteresting. As mentioned, the marketplace simply doesn't care. It only rewards results and the fair exchange for products and services produced and offered. Therefore, the understanding of the flow must be coupled with a willingness to embrace its basic tenets and work within them. Somehow, someway, no matter how creative or innovative, energy must flow out in order for it to be reciprocated. There is never a true "free lunch."

#3: The Law of Spending

"You spend money on an internet connection for your employees.
Why not spend money on the energy that fuels their brain?"
~ Shawn Anchor

As mentioned, we all have basic needs. To meet these, we will use some of the energy that we EARN (Law #2) and RECEIVE (Law #1) and we will give it back to the free market. This is the Law of SPENDING (Law #3). When you return some of your energy to the market in the form of money for products and services that you need, you participate in the flow.

Many people think: "Wait, I'm already an expert at spending."

Maybe. After your basic needs you can use your remaining energy (money) on many things. You can go to the movies. You could meet friends at a restaurant. You can head over to the mall. You can go to an amusement park. You could opt for retail therapy at your favorite shop. You can spend your money in many diverse ways.

However, there are major differences between the wealthy, the middle class and the poor and their relationship with the Law of Spending. **To EARN and RECEIVE more, you have to be worth more. To be worth more you must SPEND in intelligent ways, especially investing in the most important resource that you have which is yourself.**

The free market will give you energy based on the amount of value that you produce. The wealthy understand that when you invest in yourself and surround yourself with experts that increase your value, the free market will reward you accordingly with more energy in the form of money.

So how do the wealthy, the middle class and the poor SPEND?
The wealthy spend on assets that pay them.
The middle class spend on assets that cost them.
The poor just buy junk.
Let's break this down.

The wealthy understand that when you SPEND on yourself, to increase your ability to produce more energy, you increase the value of your greatest asset, YOU. When you SPEND to surround yourself with experts, you acquire allies that support you and increase your value. The market will then pay you with more energy based on that increased value. **When you take your energy that you EARN and RECEIVE and SPEND it intelligently, the market will return even more energy in the form of money back to you as part of the flow.**

The middle class get to the end of the month and decide that based on all the hard work they have done, they deserve an outing. They deserve a night out. They deserve new clothes. They then take themselves to their neighborhood department store and find the perfect outfit. Out comes the credit card to pay for it. In that moment, that individual acquires an asset that costs them. From that point forward it costs them every month in the form of interest. The energy of money flows away from them.

The poor simply acquire junk. How often have you walked into a room and seen a dining room shelf full of a mish-mash of assorted items, a tea-cup, a clay horse, an Eiffel tower replica all side by side-with one common element? Each of these items became instantly worthless the moment it was purchased. The $20 purchase would not get you more than .25 cents at a yard sale the very next day. How sad! The energy flow of money flat out disappears in a single transaction.

In order to achieve any measure of prosperity, we must shift our relationship with the Law of Spending and understand its rightful place in the energy flow of money. Givers spend too much when they focus only on impacting others. Connectors may not spend enough as they cherish the safety and security of keeping money to themselves. Problem Solvers can get stuck in the trees and not see the forest, thereby spending in areas that barely move the financial needle. Innovators crave change that can lead to poor decision-making with regards to spending. Perfectionists often hesitate to invest because exact results may not be predictable. Rebels gravitate to the unusual and atypical. Masters can overcomplicate a simple plan. An understanding of each Avatar's natural tendencies is critical to maintain disciplined spending habits that feed the flow.

#4: The Law of Investing

"Never stop investing. Never stop improving.
Never stop doing something new."
~ Bob Parsons

The fourth law of prosperity is by far the most important when it comes to achieving wealth. **INVESTING simply means to take some of the energy that you EARN and RECEIVE and put it to work (SPEND) in someone else's enterprise.** In exchange, that enterprise will return energy back to you in the form of dividends, increase in valuation, interest, royalties and so on.

If you take your energy and buy a share in Microsoft, then you are putting your energy to work in an enterprise started by Bill Gates. The Microsoft team is then responsible for safeguarding your energy, using it wisely and giving energy back to you in the form of dividends or increased share valuation.

If you buy into a real estate group as a passive investor, you are placing your energy in the hands of the property managers. Their function is to take your energy and develop the property so that in turn it then spins off rental income (energy) that is shared with you.

Investing is no more than placing your energy in the form of money to work somewhere else. True financial freedom comes when you have enough of your energy at work elsewhere that it generates all of the energy you need to live your desired lifestyle.

Abundant flow enables you to do what you want, when you want, with whom you choose--and to sleep well at night. What freedom! Because your Avatar drives your decision making, to get this right, you must understand how to maximize your Superpower while minimizing your Kryptonite inside the flow.

And this is particularly important because the energy flow of money is continuous.

First we must open up to RECEIVE it (Law #1).

We put our energy to work in the free market and we EARN (Law #2) energy in return that we must also RECEIVE (Law #1).

We SPEND (Law #3) a certain portion of our earned energy on necessities and the surplus can be diverted to other parts of the flow.

When we take that surplus and INVEST (Law #4), we are also SPENDING (Law #3) to put our energy back into the flow. In so doing, we open ourselves up to RECEIVING (Law #1) energy in return–right back to the beginning of the flow.

In order to fully participate in the energy flow of money, we need to first understand it. **To attain wealth, we must follow the actions of those who have paved the path before us and use our natural Superpowers to do so.** We must also avoid the pitfalls of those who participate in the flow without knowledge of its workings–and who fall easy prey to their Kryptonites. Money itself will never stop flowing.

The key wealth question becomes:

Are you building a dam and retaining your rightful share or watching your money slowly trickle away?

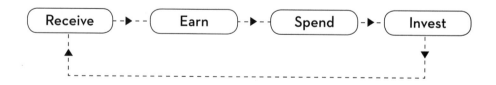

SUMMARY:

- To become prosperous, we must open our lives to Receiving, regardless of our "story" or our Kryptonite.
- Earning is the reward we receive for putting our energy to work in the marketplace.
- Spending returns a portion of our energy to the flow in exchange for products and service. The wealthy spend wisely.
- Investing is no more than putting our stored energy to work in someone else's enterprise.

CALL TO ACTION:

> Do an inventory of your habits. How do you spend? How much do you save? Are you acquiring assets? What do you invest in?

Chapter 4

YOUR AVATAR AND MONEY BASICS

"The only thing more expensive than education is ignorance."
~ Unknown source

The ideas of William Stanley Jevons who wrote the book, Money and the Mechanism of exchange, in 1875 were summed up in the following couplet:

Money's a matter of functions four,
A Medium, a Measure, a Standard, a Store.

It performs a function as a Medium of exchange.

It acts as a Measure and common denomination of trade.

It provides a Standard way of settling a debt.

It Stores value that can be used later as a Medium of exchange.

Money follows a series of fundamental tenets and in order to harness its energy, we must understand the basics, especially as they apply to the Avatars.

There are six areas that require a certain level of mastery.

The six key areas include:

1. Architecture

2. Insurance

3. Investments

4. Retirement Planning

5. Tax Planning

6. Estate Planning

1. The Architecture

"My problem lies in reconciling my gross habits
with my net income."
~ Errol Flynn

Americans are "teetering on the edge of financial disaster," affirms Greg McBride, Bankrate.com's chief financial analyst. "Not only do most of them not have enough savings, they've all used up some portion of their available credit and are running out of options."

A survey conducted by Bankrate.com confirmed this. Nearly one in four Americans have credit card debt that exceeds their emergency fund or savings. Many of them, in addition to their debt, don't have a dime in their emergency fund. A second Bankrate survey determined that 29% of Americans have no emergency savings whatsoever.

In 2014, American Express did a survey and found that half of all Americans experienced an unexpected expense in the past year. 44% had an unforeseen crisis in health care and 46% had some form of car trouble. Bad health or poor transportation can lead to far worse consequences.

Then why are so many Americans deficient in these areas? There is no shortage of advice from co-workers, financial do-it-yourself applications, online resources and articles, radio shows and online pundits that purport that you can successfully manage your own finances. The reality however is that the rich keep getting richer and the rest aren't so lucky.

Why is that?

Many of us have heard the analogy about the wrong way to build a house. You don't go out and pick up a load of bricks and some cement plus a few wooden beams and a bag of nails and then head to the property to start construction. First you create an architectural plan, establish a timeline, figure out the initial parameters and only then can you even begin to lay a foundation much less put up the walls.

Your financial plan is no different yet most Americans piecemeal the foundational items, if in fact they have a plan at all. They have a checking and a savings account, someone who prepares the tax return, a so-called investment expert and multiple little investments made on the advice of a cousin, friend or colleague in disjointed fashion. Some have a 401K or other retirement accounts and perhaps a college savings plan.

In other words, there is no cohesive plan.

The small amount of money spent on the right financial architect who has both the professional expertise and the understanding of your goals and objectives, as well as the mechanisms to get you there, can save you many thousands as you build the financial safe haven of your dreams.

Great attention must be paid to sourcing the best team–most often more than one person–to craft your strategy, trajectory, needs and milestones, as well as to consistently review your progress. Not only can most of us recognize obvious deficiencies in our own knowledge base, we don't know what we don't know–and in this area, what you don't know, will cost you.

What if your liability insurance is insufficient? Could one mistake put your entire nest egg at risk?

What if market conditions shift and your current strategy, that same one that has worked for several years in a row, has turned a negative corner and gone into a downward spiral? Do you have a system to monitor that?

How often are you reviewing your portfolio? Is your analysis rational, planned out and logic-based or emotional and sporadic?

If you don't design your life, you will fall into someone else's plan.

Do you know what they have planned for you, especially in the long term?

Not much.

Connectors who value trust, Problem Solvers who readily assimilate data and Perfectionists who thrive with systems naturally do well with good planning. Givers deviate when their plans are questioned and they don't want to say "no" to a challenger. Innovators want to tweak the plans, leading to breaks in the necessary continuity for long-term success. Rebels challenge each step and Masters add too much complexity. An awareness of these tendencies can help each Avatar self-regulate or seek out appropriate help.

SUPERPOWER STORY: Cut up the cards.

Few things create as many financial challenges for young adults as credit card debt. Bombarded with offers from credit card companies, the initial party and fun rapidly turn into dunning letters, phone calls and anxiety over a seemingly insurmountable mountain of debt.

To combat this recurring conundrum, our firm created a debt-pay-down spreadsheet that listed all of the credit cards, interest rates and balances for an individual. By populating the sheet, you could see at a glance, which debt to tackle first–with the obvious choice being to go after the highest interest rates before the others and work your way down the chain to the lowest until the debt is retired. This logic agreed with the recommendation of most financial planners.

The problem is that far more often than not, it failed.

Clients complained that they felt huge frustration at getting yet another bill from the same annoying credit card company every month with little progress. There was not enough payoff to justify the plan and eventually, most clients quit.

Emotionally, our clients simply couldn't do it. Even though the logic made complete sense, the results said otherwise.

What if we flipped the plan around?

Josh, the son of a Bellsouth executive, had the same issues of paying off credit card debt. He wanted to save for a home and an engagement ring yet could never build any cash reserves.

We analyzed all his balances and devised an 18 month timetable for being debt free–only this time, unlike ever before, we advised him to pay off the card with the LOWEST interest rate first.

Though he initially didn't agree with the plan, he trusted our counsel and followed the instructions.

Within two months, he paid off that first credit card. We met at our office for one purpose only–to memorialize the cutting up of the physical credit card. We took pictures and celebrated the success.

Although mildly confused, Josh followed the plan and went after the second card with the next lowest balance, not the card with the higher rate. He felt proud of his accomplishment and within a few months was back in the office for a second ceremony. As the small wins compounded, his confidence grew and he became more aggressive with the rest of his debt, cutting his spending and going after it.

After 14 months, the job was done. He successfully cut every card into small pieces and threw them in the trash can.

While logic told us to tackle the bigger interest rates first, emotional intelligence proved otherwise. The motivation that came from successive wins early in the process became far more important than a few percentage points in the long run. The emotional gains outweighed the finances and this method proved successful time and time again.

MORAL OF THE STORY:
In the credit card game, the scissors beat rock and paper every time.

2. Insurance

"There are worse things in life than death.
Have you ever spent an evening with an insurance salesman?"
~ Woody Allen

Most Americans grossly misunderstand the value and purpose of insurance. In essence, **insurance programs simply pool large amounts of money from many people who suffer no loss to take care of specific damage of a small number of people in that same insured pool who actually do suffer a loss.**

As a result, most people view insurance as a bill to pay, but don't enjoy paying it. It has little economic value absent the need for it after an incident, precisely when it matters most.

Insurance companies over the years have built poor reputations and low trust levels with most Americans, largely due to a disconnect in understanding. Complicated premium pricing for certain risks assumed by insurance companies determine the scope and cost of the coverage. If not understood correctly, this leads to overpayment and poor insurance selection—often covering the wrong risks or purchasing more than is needed. The fact that the insurance salesman gets paid on commission does little to bring clarity to the situation.

At the end of the day, the proper insurance builds a safety net around an individual, a family or a business that offers protection both financially and emotionally.

Here are the basic types of personal insurance that should, at the very least be understood and addressed so you have a proper safety net in place given your risk level.

1) Home Insurance

Home insurance is a property insurance designed to protect you from damages to your home or the possessions in your home. Often mortgage companies require it to safeguard you in the event of a catastrophic loss such as fire or unforeseen structural impairments. Although the risk of a large claim is relatively low, you need a safety net in place for your insurance foundation so that your financial plan never moves backwards due to an event beyond your control.

2) Car Insurance

Auto insurance is a type of property, liability, and medical coverage that shields you in the event that your car is involved in an accident. It can also defend you if the vehicle is damaged, stolen, or you face a lawsuit due to an accident. Everyone should carry car insurance. Americans often overpay or underpay their auto insurance premium because they neglect to learn the basic components of how the policy protects them from an unforeseen accident. Too many bells and whistles on your auto policy can increase premiums unnecessarily and take funds out of your monthly budget.

3) Umbrella Insurance

Umbrella insurance is an additional liability coverage and a relatively inexpensive way to protect you against an accident associated with your home, automobile, or boat. Most Americans don't understand umbrella insurance and put themselves at risk of being sued by injury to others or their property. A simple umbrella policy is an economical solution to protect your financial foundation from unforeseen catastrophe.

4) Life Insurance

Life insurance is most often purchased for two basic reasons. You either love somebody or you owe somebody. Simply speaking, buying a term policy that will cover your debts and protect your family and heirs in the event of premature death is the most economical solution. Contrast this with a permanent insurance product that builds cash value over time and is far more expensive. A term policy can cover your mortgage, children's educational needs, a family members' medical needs or offer a financial cushion to give your loved ones time to get back on their feet.

5) Health Insurance

This insurance covers basics physician visits, prescriptions and major surgeries or health scares that can be quite draining to your pocketbook. Despite the drain on cash flow, health insurance is an essential component to protecting your financial future. The appropriate type for each person or family should be looked at on a case by case basis by reviewing your ongoing medical needs, out of pocket costs, any other deductibles, and adding features such as a Health Savings Account which can have significant tax advantages.

6) Disability Insurance

Disability Insurance protects your greatest asset, which is you earning an income. Most financial plans bank on you earning a living and that plan crashes without an income to support its goals, even if the income stops for a short period of time. Group policies through work programs often cover the majority of your salary, typically one half to two thirds of your salary and are inexpensive in relation to the benefit you would receive. Getting an additional policy to cover close to 100% of your specific job occupation is often done by skilled professionals with special skills such as a surgeon that conducts operations. Some type of disability coverage will mitigate the risk, even if admittedly low, of ruining your financial plan.

7) **Long Term Care Insurance**

This is a cost outlay for many Americans near or in retirement because the cost of long term care can easily run into thousands of dollars. For this reason, it should be closely coordinated with the amount you have set aside and how that nest egg can be affected by the prolonged need for assisted medical services. Insufficient savings or an adequate long term care policy often places the burden on your adult children or other family members. Medicare covers minimal costs and only for a short period of time, making long term care a necessary insurance to avoid future financial disarray.

Rebels may eschew insurance altogether–even rebelling against that which is mandated by law. Innovators seek out cutting edge policies that may be a waste of money or worse, fail to cover basic needs. Givers put themselves last and can overlook fundamental coverage such as an umbrella policy. A Problem Solver believes that they can work out a solution to an issue when in actuality, the right insurance already covers it. Again, a heightened awareness of personal inclinations to buck the insurance system can avoid potential disasters–particularly as you move up the financial food chain. Risk mitigation just makes more sense.

Unnecessary coverage

Here are some common types of insurance that are known for being a "waste of money" and many advise to steer clear from them. Outside of specific, individual cases most Americans don't need to pay for the extra coverage.

1) **Mortgage Life Insurance**

The purpose of Mortgage Life insurance is to protect you in the event that you die and your mortgage cannot be paid. If you have sufficient term life insurance, then this is a wasteful expense you can avoid paying.

2) Critical Illness or Disease Specific Insurance

This type of insurance can be paid after a critical illness is diagnosed that covers both medical and non-medical expenses. A common example of this is cancer insurance. While good in theory and helpful if the actual occurrence were to happen, it often proves too expensive and wasteful. A proper health insurance policy can offer more economical options and cover many of the expenses associated with critical illnesses.

3) Life Insurance for Kids

Life insurance for your children can help give any family time to regroup after a death of their child. Sometimes using life insurance for children as a way for saving for their education is presented as an option. However the actuarial probability of a child death happening is quite low and the drain on your monthly cash flow can be reduced if these policies are avoided.

4) Accidental Death and Dismemberment Insurance

AD&D insurance is designed to provide funds in the event of an accidental death, loss of limbs, or even paralysis. It can overlap with life or disability insurance. While very inexpensive, the use of your funds may be better optimized by ensuring you have the right type of life and disability coverage and bypassing this supplemental coverage.

SUPERPOWER STORY:
Dangerous Waters

The practice of underwriting and insurance came out of a London coffee house in the late 1600s. Edward Lloyd (who later founded Lloyd's of London) operated an establishment where ship owners, captains and vendors gathered to procure and provide insurance for their goods. As shipping to the New World grew and goods crossed back and forth over the Atlantic, they set up systems to fund voyages, both for people and products.

Initially, venture capitalists funded trips for colonists, generally desperate individuals of lower stature in London, and provided the goods and services needed for colonization in exchange for a share in the riches found in the New World. Stories proliferated of silver and gold deposits in massive abundance and while these turned out to be exaggerated, what came to the fore was the need for a new commodity called tobacco. Europe could not get enough of it.

The process worked as follows. People with money put up the funds for a ship, its cargo and crew. The vendors and ship owners would in turn go to Lloyd's to present a detailed cargo list to other investors who convened for the purpose of taking a partial risk in the delivery of the cargo. They would sign on the cargo manifest below the listed merchandise, including the precise amount of risk they would absorb in exchange for a premium. Because of the placement of the signatures, this became known as "underwriting."

Most investors would defray their risk over numerous voyages and therefore most trips had multiple underwriters.

In the mid 1600s, a Frenchman by the name of Blaise Pascal, figured out a better approach to risk, using percentages and probabilities. He and his partner Pierre de Fermat created a series of actuarial tables for assessing and figuring out the cost of insurance.

To this day, much of what was discovered by the French governs the determination of insurance rates.

MORAL OF THE STORY:
Shared risk dramatically lessens the burden of disaster.

3. Investments

"We grow old too soon and smart too late."
~ Pennsylvania Dutch saying.

Suppose you are a great golfer, athlete and know the basics of the game. You know what clubs to use on each hole, how to account for the course slope, and can mentally calculate that a 68 must be posted on Sunday to ensure a win at the Masters. Does this give you the mental ability to attain that trophy?

Unfortunately not.

The margin between greatness and mediocrity is a matter of inches. That holds true in almost every facet of our lives.

Consider two Aussies, Jason Day and Robert Allenby. Through mid October of the 2016 season Jason Day made $9,500,000 in tournaments with an average score of 69.3 and played in 20 PGA events. That's $475,000 per tournament.

Compare that to Robert Allenby who brought in $275,000, averaged a score of 72.6–only 3 more strokes per round than Jason. He played in 25 events–25% more than Day. That's an average of $11,000 per tournament. Day made 43 times more money per event. A small advantage has a huge impact on final results.

Look at Tiger Woods or other top pros compared with the "average" pro. The numbers are strikingly similar. Are just a few less strokes per round worth $9,000,000?

The answer is yes in both business and investing. Most investors achieve either average or below average investment returns and fail to reach their financial goals.

Why?

Because they choose to become "do-it-yourselfers" and subject pivotal decisions to their own emotions.

Alternatively, they select a sub-par finance or accounting professional to manage their balance sheet.

Failure to exercise diligence and use prudent standards during times of market turbulence and uncertainty causes investors to lose sight of their objectives. Nowhere do we see this more clearly than when Avatars let their Kryptonites get the best of them.

The Problem Solver gets overwhelmed and Paralysis kicks in. He or she does nothing and takes a financial bath as a result.

The Innovator rushes to make a Change prematurely without carefully weighing the consequences and suffers an equally poor outcome.

During shaky markets most investors make the worse decisions and unfortunately can't change their misdirection until it's too late.

Average investors run for the hills and create fund outflows during periods of negative performance. Conversely, they then rush back in and create fund inflows after periods of strength. This behavior is known as performance chasing and subconsciously affects the decision making for the majority of investors, both individuals and professionals alike. As a result, seldom do individual "do-it-yourselfers" or even professional money managers experience the returns they expect or desire.

Investors are most often their own greatest enemy. Why is this?

Because the relationship between investment results is not directly tied to one's intellectual capability but rather to one's emotional intelligence. Without mastering your Kryptonite, you will revert back to behavior that will minimize your success.

KRYPTONITE STORY:
Not enough "likes..."

Mr. and Mrs. Coker brought their money to us in 2009 after being decimated by the market crash of 2008. They decided that after failing miserably at managing their own money, it was time to turn it over to professionals.

By early 2012, their portfolio had rebounded and recovered most of its value. Out of the blue, we received an unexpected call. "Liquidate our entire account immediately, please," was the order given. They intended to send all of their money to another institution as they had found the Golden Goose. Mr. Coker had a special contact who could get them into the Facebook IPO, reputed to be the largest technology IPO in history. They were about to be rich.

Our advisor tried pulling them back from the edge and we attempted everything to help them. Don't put all your eggs in one basket. Wait until after the Facebook IPO so you can let the market price stabilize. The Cokers believed that elite IPOs like Facebook had always doubled and tripled smart investors' money, so they would sell right after that happened. It was that simple for them. Despite our advice, they jumped anyway.

Later that year, the wife called again. They wanted to move their funds back to us. It seems that Wall Street's skepticism around Facebook's ability to monetize in a way that justified the price was gloomy to say the least. They sold their shares after the stock dropped over 30% out of fear of losing it all. What took them decades to build, dwindled away in a matter of months.

Sadly for the Cokers, Zuckerberg proved the street wrong. Had the Cokers held onto the stock until today, they would have tripled their initial investment. Unfortunately, like most investors, feelings and emotions influenced their reasons for both buying and selling.

MORAL OF THE STORY:
In the words of Warren Buffett: Be fearful when others are greedy and greedy when others are fearful.

4. Retirement Planning

"Living each day as if it were your last doesn't mean your last day
of retirement on a remote island. It means to live, fully,
authentically and spontaneously with nothing being held back."
~ Jack Canfield

Consider the following statistics:
- 80% of Americans believe they have not saved enough
  for "retirement."
- 70% of working Americans do not participate in a retirement
  plan through work either by choice or because it is not offered.
- 50% of couples and 70% of unmarried Americans receive
  50% or more of their income from Social Security.
- Only 30% of Americans expect to retire before age 65 compared
  to 50% of Americans when asked the same question 20 years ago.
- Workers age 50 and older plan to retire on average at age 67.

Those considering retirement are plagued by a series of nagging
questions.

How much do you need to save on a monthly basis for your retirement? How much will you need to live comfortably? How does the
inflation rate affect your earning power?

What rate of return should you use to compute the growth of your
money? What will be the cost of healthcare?

Do you need to save extra to account for emergencies?

What if you have a family history of health problems?

While these questions are certainly relevant, they fail to address the most fundamental issue with respect to retirement–the plan.

All individuals need to not only make a plan for their future but also follow it and evaluate it periodically in order to make necessary adjustments as life unfolds. Financial freedom never happens by accident. It requires design and discipline.

Would you go to a baker for meat or a butcher to buy bread? No. You go to the appropriate expert who can supply what you need. Nowhere does this apply more than with respect to retirement planning. As mentioned earlier, Emotional Intelligence plays a huge role in sticking to a well-designed retirement plan. Awareness by each individual of their Avatar's Superpower and Kryptonite makes a big difference. An understanding of both by a retirement planner can multiply your chances of creating a plan that will be complied with–and thereby lead to much greater success.

KRYPTONITE STORY: A house divided.

Nick and Kate came together in the wake of their respective divorces–both with two children from a previous marriage. Nick practiced real estate law and Kate was a schoolteacher. Interestingly, both parties had small inheritances from their parents that they intended to pass on to the kids. However, Nick's ex-wife came from a wealthy family. His children would be well taken care of no matter what.

As their assets grew, the need for a retirement plan, as well as the proper estate preparation, became more evident. As a lawyer, Nick decided that he could do the work himself to save money. He remembered his training from law school and figured that he could brush up on current law on the internet. Why pay another lawyer when he himself practiced law on a full time basis?

The couple had no issue with respect to their own inheritances. His would go to his children and hers would go to hers. The challenge came up with the money that they accumulated together, largely from real estate investments. How would that money provide for their retirement? Who would control the money after one of them passed?

After they both died, Nick wanted his kids to get more because he was the one who made the investments from his earnings. Kate felt the opposite. Her kids should get the lion's share because his kids had a separate inheritance from their mother and all kids should be made equal.

That was only fair.

Unable to reach any amicable agreement, Nick and Kate decided that with respect to their retirement plans, 401Ks and insurance proceeds, they would simply live on the funds created during their working lifetime.

Whoever then died first would leave the remaining funds to the other for their sustenance and the matter of the children was never resolved.

When Nick passed first, Kate sought her revenge. Per their agreement, almost all the money fell under her control for her retirement and she could do whatever she wanted with it–such as give it to her kids only.

MORAL OF THE STORY:
Lawyers who represent themselves have fools for clients.

5. Tax Planning

"Taxation without representation is tyranny."
~ James Otis

Let's consider the state of income taxes today and how most of us deal with them. The statistics are rather alarming:

- 99% of Americans overpay in taxes.
- 90% of taxpayers seek some form of assistance.
- 34% of those taxpayers use do-it-yourself software.
- 56% of those taxpayers seek professional advice.
- Less than 1% of Americans use a tax and investment professional that work together. These are the uber wealthy.

Most individuals as well as the overwhelming majority of companies don't do what needs to be done to help you with taxes. Taxes will affect, make or break all your other planning and assumptions.

CPAs, particularly those who claim to act as de facto CFOs for their clients have a sufficient background to interpret the three most important statements in finance and accounting–the Profit & Loss Statement, the Balance Sheet and a Statement of Cash Flows.

For the individual, these three statements translate into your Income for the Year, your Net Worth Statement, and your monthly spending–what flows in and out of your checking account.

Is your financial planner an accountant or a former corporate finance executive? If so, are they managing your finances along with your tax obligations? Unless you establish a clear collaboration between your accountant and your financial advisor, this virtually never happens. They operate in isolation from each other and you suffer the consequences. Ask a question of either party and you get half of an answer–because neither shares the expertise of the other.

Are you considering the tax implications for virtually all of your investments? Do you track realized capital gains and losses, dividends, and your cost basis, just to name a few? When you ask your financial professional directly to give you tax advice do you watch them squirm? They are not allowed to do so by law–what a conundrum.

Think about it. You make an investment based on the recommendation of your financial advisor and when you go to discuss one of the most pressing issues surrounding your investment, they can't talk to you. Under these legally mandated circumstances, unless you have your tax expert working closely with your financial advisor, you will miss deductions, make mistakes or worse, violate the tax laws.

Innovators and Rebels beware. There is a time for both changing and breaking the rules. Seldom is that time appropriate during tax planning.

KRYPTONITE STORY: Once in a great while, the taxes don't matter.

Colonel Fred Payne was the only child of Dr. Jonathan Payne, a successful eye surgeon with a profitable business in Sarasota, Florida. While Jonathan didn't object to Fred's military career, he certainly wished that his son made better choices in other areas and voiced his concerns on a regular basis. He objected when Fred wanted to divorce his first wife, Jeanne, who happened to be an emergency room nurse and objected even more when he met the reason why–Alice, a woman 16 years younger than Fred who claimed to "love a man in a uniform, especially a Marine."

Jonathan did all that he could to discourage Fred from continuing his relationship with Alice, from one-on-one conversations to articles about second marriages to not speaking for a while. None of it worked and Fred ignored his advances.

Finally, exasperated, Jonathan opted for the last resort.

"I'm not leaving my money to Alice," he said to Fred over a private father and son lunch.

"Whatever, Dad," was the only response Fred could muster.

Fred married Alice a few months later and while she and Jonathan made nice at family reunions and holidays, it was clear that no love was lost between them.

The years passed and finally, eight months before Fred's scheduled retirement from the Marine Corps, Jonathan died.

Along with a certain measure of sadness, Fred expressed the obvious questions.

"I wonder how much Dad was worth?" he voiced to Alice. "I wonder how much in taxes we're going to have to pay."

They met Jonathan's lawyer for the reading of the last will and testament.

Fred wouldn't need to worry about taxes. His father took care of that as he honored his commitment to Fred voiced so many years ago.

Nothing. Fred would get nothing, as long as Alice was alive–and she was a lot younger than him. Jonathan locked his fortune up into an irrevocable trust and unless Alice predeceased him, Fred would never see a penny.

MORAL OF THE STORY:
If you aren't involved and don't know the plan, you won't find out until the benefactor is dead.

6. Estate Planning

"Goal setting is bringing the future into the present
by what you do now."
~ Zig Ziglar

When it comes to wasted money, few areas suffer more than estate planning. The lack of attention to this critical area causes untold anguish as the fruits of an entire lifetime of work evaporate, end up in the wrong hands or get chewed up by legal fees. Consider the following:

- 55% of adult Americans die without a will or formal estate plan.
- 27% of those without a will or estate plan believe that this is not an urgent need.
- 15% of the population say they don't need one at all.
- 3-7% of the total assets that go into probate are paid out to cover court costs, appraisals, personal representative fees, surety bonds, and legal and accounting fees.
- Less than 3% of Americans discuss and implement an estate plan with their financial planner.

The disasters that stem from poor estate planning or none whatsoever range across a broad spectrum. The court appoints who they deem fit to watch over minor children and their money. Valuable family assets are inadvertently liquidated because an estate is "cash poor." Spendthrift loved ones receive sums of cash and burn through them only to wind up poor and destitute. Courts appoint individuals to make healthcare decisions when you are incapacitated–including when to pull the plug on your life support.

Think about that. **Someone you have never met and who knows nothing about you and your world views has control over your life or death because you failed to provide proper instructions. Even your own family has little say in the matter–all because of a lack of planning.**

What if each Avatar used their Superpowers to elevate estate planning to a new level? Givers create impacts through proper estate planning, while simultaneously giving to family and grandchildren, as well as charities and foundations. Connectors ensure that money they hold closely goes to those with the best understanding of meaningful relationships. Perfectionists gain solace by implementing an airtight, structured plan that provides a predictable outcome and level of certainty for them and their heirs. The Innovator becomes a kid in a candy store when they learn about creative possibilities such as CRUTs, QTIPs, QPRTs, QDOTs, GRUTs, and countless other estate planning strategies to preserve and grow wealth. Problem Solvers and Masters take on the challenge of understanding the complexities of how one effectively passes on their wealth to those they care most about. What a difference being self-aware of your Avatar has on estate planning!

Regardless of your Kryptonite, unless you provide for your estate, someone else will decide what happens to it–and one thing is certain, as a matter of law the government will reach deeply into your pocket wherever possible. Do you really want to make an unnecessary gift to Uncle Sam?

KRYPTONITE STORY:
Famous Last Words.

"Jacob, this money is yours and I want you to use it for your children." Uncle Brent uttered his last words to his nephew on his deathbed. Jacob felt close to his Uncle Brent and now their time together finally came to an end. Jacob never knew about, nor expected to receive any life insurance proceeds when

Uncle Brent passed–so these words came as quite a surprise. Uncle Brent never had children and this was his way of leaving his legacy to his trusted nephew.

Regrettably, Brent never followed through with the proper paper-work. He made a call to his insurance company after his divorce from Aunt Sarah but the insurance beneficiary was never formally changed. Even though Brent's will stated that the life insurance should go to his nephew, Aunt Sarah, long since divorced from Brent, still remained on the policy. A simple signature would have been all that was required. Jacob and his children, received nothing.

MORAL OF THE STORY:
The road to hell is paved with good intentions.

SUMMARY:

- These six money fundamentals encompass your complete financial plan: Architecture, Insurance, Investments, Retirement Planning, Taxation and Estate Planning.
- An overwhelming number of Americans have no cohesive plan, a state that can lead to horrendous consequences.
- Success leaves clues. The only secure way to attain wealth is to do what the wealthy do and assemble a team that includes experts in each of the fundamental areas. Do-it-yourselfers simply cannot attain a sufficient level of mastery in all areas.

CALL TO ACTION:

Review your current team. Who helps you to draft your financial plan? Who handles your insurance? Who selects and manages your investments? Do they work with your tax person? Have you completed a Retirement Plan? How about an Estate Plan–are your Wills and/or Trusts in order?

Chapter 5

HOW DO YOU AND YOUR PARTNER DEAL WITH MONEY?

Where Kryptonites collide and fortunes disappear... Why most couples go broke and so few succeed.

"The foundation of a financial fresh start actually
has nothing to do with money or specific financial dos and don'ts.
The first, and most difficult step is to absolve yourself
and your spouse or partner of any guilt."

~ Suze Orman

"I like you."

From a psychological standpoint, what that means most often is: "I like you because I am a lot like you."

We feel uncomfortable around those who are "different" than what we are used to and understand. We make snap judgments about others with no filter but our own when considering who someone else might be–though in truth we know virtually nothing about them. Hence there are those that you "naturally get along with" and those that "are not really your type"– (which translates as "you really can't stand…")

From the perspective of your Avatar, there are certain Avatars that you "naturally get along with" and others where that is not the case at all. In fact, in the absence of knowing the Avatar of another person, the potential for conflict is ripe, immediate and can be devastating in a relationship.

How often have you had the feeling "I just don't get them" OR "I can't relate to them?" The extension of that thought is "…and therefore if they leave me alone and stay with their friends and away from mine, we'll do just fine."

What about your partner or spouse? They say that opposites attract. Have you ever stopped to think about why?

It makes total sense. You have a Superpower and a Kryptonite. You meet someone with a completely different Superpower.

How alluring and intriguing. The attraction is obvious and immediate. This Avatar has a Superpower that is so different from yours. They have something that you don't.

You ask yourself: "Could I get some of that? Could I learn from it? Could I increase my own power in some way?"

 Imagine a Connector who expends much energy to build a safe and trusting environment. She excels at creating a protected and sheltered space for those she cares about most.

She meets a Rebel who lives outside the box. How exciting! How can he do that? His Superpower is to Challenge everything? How mysterious and captivating!

Initially, the glamor and temptation of something so opposite carry the day and the Connector ventures into the Rebel's space. Though puzzling and perplexing, it's all so new and electric.

Then the Rebel's Kryptonite kicks in. He begins to isolate. He challenges everything the Connector thinks, says and does.

Also imagine that neither of them know their own Avatar nor the

Avatar of this new energy. How long will they last? How soon before an explosion drives them apart or worse, they begin to put out the initial flames and cancel out each other's Superpower?

She begins to take unnecessary risks against everything she believes in. He "settles" in ways that extinguish his flame, without even realizing it. The Superpowers fog up and become obscured, each overshadowed by the other with no guidance on how to bring out their light.

What if instead, the Connector and the Rebel understood each other completely? They know of their own unique Superpowers and how those come to life.

The Connector appreciates that when the Rebel challenges something and greater clarity emerges, it actually builds trust (as opposed to breaking it down–which is exactly what happens without understanding the Rebel's motivation for challenging.)

The Rebel embraces that in a safe environment, he can allow his nature to run free on a greater metaphysical level—that a trusting space takes his ability to challenge to new heights.

Mutual respect develops. The Superpowers complement rather than collide with each other. United, they cover both sides of most issues, the daring and risk taking aspect of the Rebel balanced by the refuge and conservative nature of the Connector.

An understanding of your Avatar and that of your partner can alter the course of a relationship—take it to both new depths based on awareness and new heights based on the compounding effect of diverse Superpowers.

By contrast, a lack of understanding, particularly about how Kryptonites collide, can cause a lifetime of pain and unhappiness. This, of course, translates into poor decisions about money as each person seeks to "stand their ground" or "hold their turf" as opposed to uniting toward common objectives.

Even a competent financial planner will have grave difficulty bringing a couple together if neither of them know how the other views the world based on their Avatar.

In fact, they likely have preconceived notions about the other based on their own Avatar that are not at all in line with their partner's views. It is a recipe for communication disaster and misunderstandings galore–certainly making it exceedingly more difficult to properly execute a financial plan of any kind–no matter who creates it or administers it.

KRYPTONITE STORY: On a Roll...

All Lisa needed was a new set of tires. Who knew this would cause the fight of the century between her and her husband Roger. They both made healthy incomes. They drove luxury cars. They lived in a nice home with a picket fence and a sycamore tree that dropped tons of leaves to the delight of their golden retriever, affectionately named Rhett Butler. College educated and seemingly successful, they epitomized the urban family.

"You spend too much money shopping for clothes and knick knacks," was Roger's first poke. He felt frustrated with the situation at hand though wasn't all that serious about his comment–more of a token jab. Even if it did cost a bit more money, he enjoyed seeing his Lisa bubbly and more lively when she wore her stylish attire to work and out on the town. Still that was all it took to get the fire started.

"You spend too much on golf and stupid stuff from Alabama," she shot back. "The Tide are going to roll us all the way off a cliff. You're on what–your 10th or so commemorative championship set?"

That was a hurtful and low blow to a college football fanatic from the South. Challenging his loyalty to his alma mater generally stood off limits and Lisa knew it. She simply defended herself from his remarks and did not feel all that serious about her comment either. She actually enjoyed the down time when Roger and his friends spent fall Saturdays consumed by their college football ritual. Nonetheless, that's all it took to kick the fight up to another level.

Roger fought back to defend his "reasonable" purchases. After all, most of Roger's friends had entire rooms set up to watch and commemorate Alabama football. "Most of my friends think you are dating either Jimmy Choo or Michael Kors" he contended.

This same pattern repeated itself month-on and month-off since they got married. Even though they seemed to make up shortly thereafter, it still caused quite a bit of unrest on the weekends when they could be relaxing and enjoying each others' company. Those one-off expenses were not in their budget and therefore not planned for. Lisa and Roger both felt like they were reasonable with their personal spending despite the lack of planning. Now a senseless argument came about because Lisa needed a set of new tires and they had to put it on the credit card. The money wasn't in their checking account, so what could they do?

They tried to follow a structured budget which they casually addressed every 6 months or so. They contributed to their retirement plans through work. They balanced their checking account. What were they doing wrong?

Any small surplus of money in their checking account gave them a false sense of security and more importantly a subconscious affirmation that they could spend that money. They fell victim to their own success. They made plenty of money. Why shouldn't they spend it? That's what a checking account is for–to write checks. So what if they lived paycheck to paycheck?

They didn't need an estate plan. There was nothing left to plan for.

MORAL OF THE STORY:
If you don't stem the Tide of spending, the only way you Roll is into insolvency.

Communication is key
Are you lighting the path or living in the dark?

In the absence of knowing your partner's Avatar, their very nature can drive a chasm into your relationship–especially when it comes to communication. Givers and Connectors are largely emotional and feeling based. Problem Solvers, Innovators and Perfectionists are far more analytical and thinking based. The Rebel lives outside the box completely and the Master abides in a highly cerebral place where others tend not to relate.

With regard to money, the challenges multiply.

The Giver believes in generosity–what if your partner doesn't?

The Connector wants to play it safe–what if your partner doesn't believe that approach will ever get you anywhere financially?

The Problem Solver can see the immediate solution and drive to move quickly–what if your partner needs more time and consideration to make a decision?

The Innovator embraces change readily–what if your partner simply doesn't?

The Perfectionist needs the ducks to line up in a perfect row– what if your partner could care less?

The Rebel will challenge even your financial planner–with your blessing or without.

The Master can overcomplicate a basic plan–what if your partner needs no extra knowledge whatsoever to move forward?

All of these challenges are solved if both parties know and understand their Avatars.

When people know their Avatars, even if they disagree on a point, they understand where the other person is coming from. They can appreciate the difference in point of view without getting "plugged in" or feeling the need to be right.

A healthy discussion can ensue with multiple options available for exploration as opposed to two individuals stuck in a narrow perspective and looking to defend it.

With respect to money which can undoubtedly be a highly charged issue, both the upside potential and the downside risk increase. If a couple understands each other's Avatar, the Superpowers compound and a healthy dialogue can broaden both perspectives–especially when facilitated by a financial professional.

On the other hand, **when Kryptonites collide in the absence of understanding–because every couple's Kryptonites are alive and well whether they know them or not–this can have disastrous consequences.**

Hurt feelings, lack of empathy, outright fights and total disconnects between the parties commonly occur. Even financial advisors make little progress when two partners cannot see eye to eye based on a lack of understanding, which obviously translates beyond the relationship and into finances. Communication can turn into a nightmare.

KRYPTONITE STORY:
All she wants is a card.

Morrie Schwartz and his wife Evelyn were on their third psychiatrist in three years, a woman named Barbara.

From Morrie's perspective, this whole "go see a shrink" thing was a complete waste of money and as a self-made wealthy man, nothing bothered him more. To suggest that he acted uncooperatively was an understatement, a fact that bothered Evelyn tremendously as she believed that he didn't really care about their marriage.

Their first two meetings deteriorated into a fight about Evelyn's birthday.

"I got her a diamond," Morrie began. "A nice one."

"I didn't want a diamond," Evelyn retorted. "I already have a lot of diamonds."

"How could she not want a diamond?" Morrie talked about Evelyn in the third person, directing his comments to Barbara. "All women like diamonds."

"I told you that I didn't want another diamond," Evelyn implored. "All I wanted was a card. A nice card from you."

Morrie ignored her. "Can you believe that? I get her a diamond and she complains."

Barbara tried in vain to intervene. "Did you ask her what she wanted?"

"What's to ask?" Morrie rambled. "I've been married for almost 30 years and I know she likes diamonds. So I got her one. And this is the thanks I get."

"But did you talk to her about her desires, Morrie?" Barbara insisted.

"It's her birthday. A gift is supposed to be a surprise. I surprised her."

"It's useless, Barbara, like I told you," Evelyn sighed, dejected. "He never listens. All I wanted was a simple card."

MORAL OF THE STORY:
Diamonds may not be forever after all.

Natural Matches

Which Avatars see the world in similar ways? Who are the people likely to get along and how do we determine that?

Simple. Look at the Superpowers. Those that complement each other will naturally give rise to similar temperaments and views that make it easy to get along and relate. In addition, those that don't compete or threaten one another, while perhaps not as strong of a natural match, reduce conflict and separation–thereby leading to common understanding.

Let's break this down.

The Giver, whose Superpower is Cause(s) will get along fairly well with the Problem Solver, who excels at solutions. Contributing to causes goes along with creating solutions so while this is not a perfect match, neither does it create conflict.

The Giver will also empathize with the Master who seeks depth as a Superpower. The deeper you go, the more you can give.

The Connector who constantly builds Trust, much like the Giver, will get along well with the Problem Solver inasmuch as Solutions lead to greater Trust. However, to an even greater degree the Connector fits hand in glove with the Perfectionist who builds Systems and does things right–a perfect way of establishing and growing Trust–even more so than the Problem Solver.

The Problem Solver, in addition to the Giver and Connector, establishes quick affinity with the Master who seeks Depth. Obviously greater Depth will give rise to even more Solutions or better Solutions. The Superpowers complement each other.

The Innovator and the Rebel use their Superpower to seek change. Hence a kinship forms naturally as they, for their own unique reasons, want something different. The Innovator strives for Improvements. The

Rebel looks to Challenge the norm or convention. This combination creates explosive creativity that is exciting to both.

While all of the above combinations give birth to natural matches, the more important point is the following:

Any two Avatars can multiply their Superpowers as long as they both know and embrace the strength of the other. This applies to finances as well as all other aspects of a relationship.

It is only in the absence of this knowledge that conflicts run rampant.

KRYPTONITE STORY:
Different strokes for different folks...

Kat and Rog (short for "Kathleen" and "Roger") have diametrically opposed views of money. Rog makes a lot of it as a top salesman, with an occasional dry spell that he calls a "cold streak" that only seems to come around once every couple of years.

By contrast, Kat works as a school teacher and sets her paychecks up on a twelve month cycle even though she doesn't work in the summer, just so that she can do better budgeting. This enables her to take the summer months off to visit family and focus on her garden.

When they first began dating, all seemed well. They did things out of the ordinary for both of them and it was exciting because they were so different. Kat liked Rog's panache and he was drawn to her stability. They seemed to magnify and compliment each other in some odd way.

As the relationship intensified however, their differences escalated with it.

Kat hated to spend money and would certainly never buy anything at retail. If she couldn't find a coupon or a promotion, forget it–she would wait until an item went on sale.

Rog thought she could "suck a dime out of a nickel" as he expressed to his brother over drinks. He felt she was way too stingy.

When Rog bought a new convertible, rather than acting excited, Kat thought it was absurd that he paid full price. Why didn't he get a second hand model? Didn't he know that the car lost 30% of its value the minute he drove it off the lot?

They began to feel resentment towards each other, despite the fact that at least for a while, the "M" word crept into their vocabulary. How could they ever get married with such opposite perspectives? Kat wanted stability. Rog craved experiences–and the best ones definitely cost a few bucks.

Fortunately, a friend introduced them to the Avatars which gave them a better understanding of each other. Kat is a Connector and as such values trust above all else. Rog is a Problem Solver and to him, the ability to make money is simply a by-product of offering solutions to obvious problems or situations–which is exactly what a good salesman does.

As their awareness of each other grew, so did the mutual respect and empathy, even though neither of them wanted to change who they were. Kat would always be frugal. Rog relished his role as the "King of Fun."

That same friend suggested a pre-nup and a budget that allowed each of them to continue to be themselves. Kat would keep her small portfolio of investments and Rog would keep his toys. Going forward, each of them would contribute 60% of their earnings to the family budget and could do whatever they wanted with the rest. Kat could grow her portfolio with her 40% and Rog could plan great experiences for both of them to share with his 40%–a win-win for everyone.

Though it took a while for the couple to settle into these parameters, they played to each of their strengths, to their Superpowers, and in short order magnifying each other became part of their routine.

A few months later they had a beautiful honeymoon largely paid for by Rog–even though the cost was well outside of Kat's comfort zone.

MORAL OF THE STORY:
While opposites may attract, maximizing Superpowers forges bonds that transcend stereotypes and lead to great strength.

Likely Combatants

What about the opposite of natural matches?

Which Avatars quickly clash and either battle or run from each other?

How do we figure out why and how those dynamics work?

Just as simple. Look to the Kryptonites. Kryptonites that support or perpetuate an issue hold those Avatars back and cause separation. Kryptonites that collide in a big way and either accelerate or exacerbate an issue have the potential to rub each other raw in a hurry–with all sorts of negative consequences.

Let's consider some of the likely combatants.

The Giver's Kryptonite is Over-Commitment. Therefore any of the Avatars that values completion and precision will have issues with this. The Connector, who because of their emotional nature might be thought to get along well with the Giver, can have a serious challenge when the Giver's Over-Commitment leads to dropped balls, shoddy work or mistakes–all challenges that threaten Trust.

The Perfectionist who values things done right and struggles with Rigidity, will have an even greater problem with the Giver's failure to deliver, both properly and in a timely fashion.

The Connector will clash with any Avatar that threatens Trust. In addition to the Giver when they Over-Commit, the Connector will take issue with the Innovator's constant need for Change and even more so with the Rebel's desire to Challenge everything.

When the Master overcomplicates a matter, this too, can lead to Trust breakdowns.

The Innovator is a harbinger for Change. Hence, Avatars that prefer safety, security and systems, such as the Connector and Perfectionist, will clash frequently.

The Perfectionist's Rigidity will face challenges with the Innovator and their penchant for Change, with the Rebel and their desire to

Challenge and with the Master who creates Complexity.

The Rebel, naturally Challenges everyone. Their Kryptonite of Isolation cuts both ways. They isolate themselves when others don't agree and others will push them away when they feel threatened.

Despite the potential for frequent breakdowns and relationship damage, the oft repeated adage in this work plays out with respect to Kryptonites more than anywhere.

If each Avatar knows the Superpower and Kryptonite of each other, none of the habitual behavior comes as a surprise or feels threatening. While perhaps a tad annoying at times, mutual respect for known differences can overcome the separation, breakdown and conflict that stem from a lack of understanding.

In fact, seeing any issue from a totally different perspective, can prove quite rewarding and expansive. Imagine your partner expanding your view of profit potential, improving your saving or spending habits, supporting your moving of the financial needle. What a difference compared to the bickering and finger pointing so prevalent today.

 KRYPTONITE STORY: Hey, Big Spender...
When Elise watched Brad drive up in a brand new Porsche she understood why he insisted on picking her up. At such a young age, few people had a car like that and even though it set off warning signals, she ignored them. Brad had a good job, obviously made more than she did and seemed like a really nice guy.

She didn't give much thought a few dates later when she agreed to go back to Brad's place and found out it was in one of the nicest neighborhoods in town, in a fancy high rise with a doorman. Though it seemed odd that he insisted on paying for everything, she reaped the benefits and quickly stopped worrying about it.

After a few months, Elise moved in with Brad and half a year later, he asked her to marry him. Their conversations around money were vague and obtuse and Elise didn't want to rock the boat. She had a job and her own money in any case and because she paid for little else, was able to buy nice things for her fiancee that he appeared to greatly appreciate.

As their wedding day approached, she couldn't bring herself to interrupt their bliss with a topic as distasteful as money. Somehow, bills were handled and she had far more important things to worry about–like a dress for herself and her bridesmaids.

After a lavish honeymoon, Elise felt that she had the right to review their finances and while she didn't start probing or delving into Brad's old files, she did take a look at the ongoing correspondence, only to find out that Brad carried massive amounts of credit card debt–on multiple cards. The Porsche was leased at almost $1000 per month and their rent cost $2700. Everything Brad possessed topped the end of the expense spectrum, from the internet package to the cable bill to the membership at the high-end gym down the street–even though their building had its own workout room. She couldn't believe it. Aghast, she called her mother for advice.

"If he's been this way since you've known him, he'll be this way his whole life," her mother counseled. "You have to ask yourself whether you can live with that."

Even as a newlywed, Elise felt unsure. Brad's ideas about money went against everything she stood for and believed in. His "relax and enjoy life" attitude frustrated her beyond belief. What about the future, responsibility and saving for a rainy day? Brad simply didn't care–except that now, they were a family. She began to worry about being responsible for Brad's bills. What if the credit card companies started calling her?

Every dollar Brad made was earmarked ahead of time–just a matter of which bill did it pay. There was no cushion, no safety net and no plan–and no real desire to create one–at least not on Brad's part.

Slowly, Elise felt herself drifting away from Brad. He was so different from her. What initially started out as attraction morphed into quiet disdain. He didn't get it and wasn't going to change. Almost two years to the day of their wedding, she moved out and filed for divorce.

Brad never understood why.

MORAL OF THE STORY:
In the words of Napoleon Hill: "Money without brains is always dangerous."

SUMMARY:

- Certain Avatars naturally get along while others clash with equal ease.
- When couples know each others Avatars, they understand where the other person is coming from and can appreciate their differences in points of view without feeling the need to be right.
- With understanding, Avatars can multiply their Superpowers and play to each other's strengths.
- Without understanding, Kryptonites will drive wedges between the most well-intentioned relationships.

CALL TO ACTION:

Do you know and understand your partner's Avatar?
If not, what are you waiting for? The road to a better relationship stretches out right in front of you.

Chapter 6

HOW DO YOUR KIDS RELATE TO MONEY?

Will they grow it or squander it away?

"It's easier to build strong children than to repair broken men."
~ Frederick Douglass

"Where does money come from?"– a standard question that sooner or later is asked of a youngster.

"From Mommy and Daddy," tends to be the pat answer.

And why should they think differently–unless of course we choose to educate them.

If we know the Avatars of our children, then we have a general sense of their tendencies and in turn can tailor programs to optimize their Superpower and perhaps more importantly, minimize their Kryptonite.

When it comes to money and children, one thing stands firm. Our own behavior around money will influence them more than words ever will. It's a matter of not only talking the talk–we must also walk the walk.

And of course, our children's perspective will change dramatically in a short amount of time–largely based on our example.

Phase 1:
The Early Years from 0 to 5.
A Time of Imprinting.

"Early childhood education is the key
to the betterment of society."
~ Maria Montessori

Early experimentation shapes the Avatars of our children. They have needs and wants and don't consciously know how to have them met.

Initially, they cry. When they get what they need, they do it again. And again. And again.

Success breeds success...why not keep doing what works?

Until finally, parents wake up one day and declare: "Stop. Crying will not work anymore. You can't get what you want by screeching ever again."

Famous last words. Although, in this moment, a shift definitely happens.

The kids must try new behavior, different actions to have their needs and wants met.

So they do. Each time a new action fails, they discard it as useless. When it succeeds, they try it again. If it works, they repeat it. Again and again.

Slowly yet steadily, without any conscious knowledge, they build a belief system. "If it works, repeat. If not, discard."

Like tiny wire filaments that in isolation hold up nothing, as the single wires wrap around each other based on repeated successes, they form a belief system, a process of activity that justifies their behavior–an Avatar.

Initially, it's how they survive. For those who embrace the beliefs, it's how they thrive.

Eventually, those tiny filaments number in the hundreds and then thousands and form a massive cable strong enough to hold up the Golden Gate Bridge.

Your belief system manifests as your Avatar.

At an early age children are most impressionable. Based on the formation of their Avatar, the impressions last for a lifetime.

How critical is it, therefore, to do everything possible to make those influences lasting and value creating?

How important is it for all parents to have an understanding of the Avatars of their children?

SUPERPOWER STORY:
Positive money imprints.
Camille's father offered her a fun job. She would be the "money educator" on her Dad's financial webinars that he held periodically online in the evenings and would be paid $5 for each presentation. In order to qualify for the job, she had to memorize a certain script. It went like this.

DAD:	"Camille–what is money?"
CAMILLE:	"It's energy, Dad."
DAD:	"And what else is it?"
CAMILLE:	"It's a financial instrument."
DAD:	"What's a bank?"
CAMILLE:	"A place where you save money."
DAD:	"What's a profit?"
CAMILLE:	"That's when you buy something and sell it for more."
DAD:	"Is a profit good?"
CAMILLE:	"Very good, Dad."

DAD:	"What's a debt?"
CAMILLE:	"That's when you borrow money."
DAD:	"Is a debt good?"
CAMILLE:	"Not usually, Dad."
DAD:	"How do you want to live, Camille?"
CAMILLE:	"Debt-free, Dad."
DAD:	"Thank you, Camille–go brush your teeth and get ready for bed, please."

Camille presented on her first webinar at age 5 and continued to do so for a number of years. The imprint of living "debt-free" will stay with her forever.

MORAL OF THE STORY:
How much better would your children's finances be if they lived "debt-free"?

Phase 2:
The Formative Years from 6-10.
A Time of Seeding.

"How one handles success or failure is determined
by their early childhood."
~ Harold Ramis

The formative years mold the Avatar into what it will always be. During this period, kids begin to develop their belief system, even if unconsciously.

What used to be: "Crying gets me milk" morphs into "If I'm nice, this happens...If I'm clever, this happens...If I shut up, this happens...If I speak out, this happens..." and so on.

The experimentation continues and in the process, the locking down of beliefs and systems of belief naturally follow.

During this period, the behavior of the parent is paramount in shaping the children. Their Avatars are becoming more and more solidified. Children need to do what they do to survive–even in an environment where survival can mean getting what they want, avoiding a beating or winning over a sibling.

For a young child, it's all the same–at least when it comes to the formation of their Avatar. One single filament of belief at a time, shapes and molds the whole.

The actions and reactions of the parent during this period play a pivotal role. To the child, approval or disapproval often signals the difference between success and failure–and the keeping or discarding of a belief filament.

Everything matters, especially when you consider that their Avatar, once formed, will guide and influence every single action they take for the rest of their life.

We can all benefit from reminding ourselves of the old saying:

"Shhh. You don't need to say anything. Your actions speak so loudly I can't hear you."

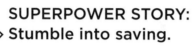

SUPERPOWER STORY:
Stumble into saving.

Every Saturday, Hudson, age 7 and Deacon, age 6 hold a financial meeting with their father. They keep a black journal that tracks their earnings, savings, and withheld taxes–like their own little payroll vendor. Each has their own money box labeled with their name and "Banco de Daddy." In it they keep their cash and some valuable coins gifted to them by family and close friends. Each of the boys lock their own box in a drawer where their banker (Dad) grants access upon request. Every week they fill out the journal together as they discuss weekly progress and their current financial situation. During the meeting Dad asks a series of questions about the recent week.

"What chores did you do this week?"

"How were you nice to each other?"

"What did you do to show love to each other?"

"How did you pay attention at school and how were you respectful to your teachers and classmates?"

"What did you learn at school that would make Mommy and Daddy proud?"

"How did you behave for Mommy while Daddy was at work?"

"What did you do that might make Daddy sad? How are you going to try to make sure that doesn't happen again?"

Dad keeps the questions open ended so that the boys think for themselves, each seated in a chair facing Dad's desk. Upon finishing the first part of the meeting, Dad hands each of them their weekly allowance of $20 and begins a new round of questions with an entirely different spin.

"How much will you put in savings?"

"25%" they say as they pass over $5 dollars. Although they haven't learned percentages yet, they memorized the amount after the first few meetings.

"How much do you pay in taxes?"

"25%" they reply and hand over another $5 dollars.

"How much do you have left?"

"$10 dollars," they answer.

"Do you want to spend it or save it?"

They each choose between spending that money by keeping it in their wallet (checking account) or saving it by depositing it in "Banco de Daddy". Once deposited it cannot be withdrawn unless it is for an impactful life purchase.

Initially, the boys chose to spend their money until one day, Hudson blurted out:

"Save it!"

Deacon seemed perplexed at this choice. How would his brother get any candy or buy those wanted toys?

A week later, Deacon followed suit and saved his money, too. Was this responsibility they were learning? Not at all. What began impetuously, turned into a rivalry. Who could save the most money? Who could win the competition?

Regardless of original motive, they now made new choices, of their own volition.

"Save it!" became the mantra, even before the question could be fully voiced.

If only more adults felt the same way...

MORAL OF THE STORY:
Good habits built young will influence a lifetime.

The relativity of money.

> "You have to teach children about money intentionally–
> create teachable moments." ~ Dave Ramsey

A 50% off sale proves less of a driver for kids. When they see an ad for a sale on Legos and think it's a good deal, what they see is the ad, not the discounted value. A great commercial that advertises a 1% discount off all Legos products will likely have the same effect on a 5 year old as a 99% off sale. Children who buy the items they want with their own money appreciate its value at an earlier age. When those purchased toys are tossed aside within a few days, they learn through experience.

When children earn their own spending money they grasp the value of goods by being able to afford or not afford (telling them they haven't saved enough money) certain items.

Not allowing them to buy what they want because they spent the money elsewhere facilitates the learned behavior. It strongly sets the groundwork to earlier understand that there is no such thing as a free lunch.

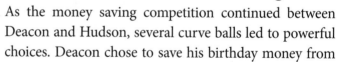

FOLLOW UP: SUPERPOWER STORY #2: Competition breeds understanding.

As the money saving competition continued between Deacon and Hudson, several curve balls led to powerful choices. Deacon chose to save his birthday money from Gigi and Pops thereby upsetting his brother, Hudson, who became unclear as to how he could ever catch up.

Dad finally reminded him that he, too, had a birthday upcoming.

A few weekends later, Deacon, knowing he was ahead and before the financial meeting, decided to spend his extra $10 dollars on a game. Hudson immediately glanced at Dad with triumph in his eyes because he knew that with his birthday money from Gigi and Pops he would take a solid lead.

At the end of the year Dad took them through a process to experience how much they earned over the year and what implications those earnings have.

"How much did you earn over the past year by doing work and chores?" Dad asked.

"25%" they responded.

"How much did you withhold for taxes?" Dad continued.

"25%" they responded again.

Dad counted out the money as the boys watched bug-eyed as the stack of dollar bills piled up.

"You set this money aside every week because you have to pay taxes to the IRS every year," Dad explained.

Almost unconsciously, the progress of building earnings over the year begins to resonate.

The boys then take an envelope, insert the money, address it to the IRS, and walk it to the mailbox. The first time they put the money in the envelope, they felt sad and disappointed–a perfect moment for the next conversation!

"Why do you think you are paying the government this money that you worked so hard for?

"To help poor people!" Deacon blurted out, a comment heard in school, or at Bible study.

"That's definitely part of it," Dad acknowledged. "What about the roads we drive on? Who pays for those? And what about the red lights on those roads? And the school buses that take kids to school? And Uncle Eric who takes care of bad guys as a policeman? And the soldiers that fly overseas to protect our country?"

As the questions sink in, the light bulb goes off for both of them.

"OK," they both voice as they trot the envelope to the mailbox, proud of their contribution.

MORAL OF THE STORY:
In the words of Author, Jess Lair: "Children are not things to be molded, but people to be unfolded."

Phase 3:
The Adolescent Years from 11-15.
A Time of Nurturing.

"I can't think of anything I'd rather do with my money
than buy my children the best possible education."
~ Niall Ferguson

By the time a child crests north of 10 years old, their Avatar begins to take hold. They have a broad array of experiences, both victories and failures that shape how they approach each decision–a mental programming that manifests on a daily basis through their Avatar.

Knowing the Avatar with certainty will give you an enormous influence over your child's behavior and a much greater ability to help them make better decisions–including maximizing their Superpower and gaining awareness of their Kryptonite.

Here's the challenge. Many adolescents either don't know how to express their Avatar or will resist the process. They are far too concerned with peer pressure, saying the right thing or not saying the wrong one and feel generally resistant to being vulnerable with a parent. As they approach puberty and begin the separation process, the gap broadens–as is the natural order.

So what can you do?

Nurture.

Experiment.

Let them try things.

Encourage them.

Remember that for them, "love" is spelled "T-I-M-E".

Sooner than you think, they will have very little time for you. **While you are still perceived as a hero, act like one.**

SUPERPOWER STORY: Surf's Up!

Linus approached his father a few months into late spring. "Dad–I'll be thirteen this summer," he began.

"That's right," Dad replied. "You'll finally be a teenager."

"I know what I want for my birthday," Linus continued.

"Oh?"

"A surfboard," Linus paused. "I mean a real one."

"That's nice," Dad answered. "And how much does a 'real one' cost?"

"Around $200," Linus stated.

His father paused for a moment. "And how badly do you want this surfboard?"

"Big time," Linus exclaimed. "I've been practicing and I'm good enough to get out there with the older kids."

"So you want this surfboard by your birthday in August so you can join the big boys before summer ends?" Dad mused.

"That's right. I'd like you to buy it for me for my birthday."

"How about if I help you get it? Would that be alright?" Dad asked. "As long as you get the board, you'll be happy, right?"

"Yes, sir," Linus declared.

"Okay, son," Dad pointed to the dining room table. "Let's make a business plan." He grabbed a legal pad and a pen.

"What do you mean, Dad?" Linus said with a funny look.

"I'm not buying you a $200 surfboard. I will however, help you get it yourself."

"How are you going to do that?" Linus queried.

"We have a big trip to see relatives in a month and we're going to make a plan to ensure that you earn $200 for your surfboard." He pushed the pad across the table. "At the top, title this 'Linus' surfboard plan'. Then write down all the things that you can do to make money."

"What do you mean, Dad?" Linus began to adopt a surly tone.

"Just what I said. You can mow grass, wash cars, walk dogs and so on. Write down everything you can think of." Dad crossed his arms.

"I'm serious. You'll see. Do what I ask."

Yard work. Poop pick-up. Painting. Car washing. Weeding. Trash removal. Dog walking. Pet sitting. Raking. Sweeping.

The list grew quickly.

"Excellent," Dad said. "Now put a price on each of the services that you offer."

"I don't get it, Dad," Linus pouted.

"It's not complicated. How much do you charge to walk a dog, rake a yard, wash a car? Write your fees down next to each service."

Linus reluctantly complied.

"Good job," Dad said, patiently seated across the table. "Now, on a separate piece of paper jot down your potential clients. Make a list of every single person you are likely to see over the next three months before your birthday."

"Like who, Dad?" Linus blurted, with a bit of an attitude.

"Every single adult you can think of, Linus. Start from where we are this week, think about the trip we're going on and include every adult–Uncle Clark, Granpuff, Mr. and Mrs. Jones–everyone. Go month by month and write their names down."

"This is kind of bogus, Dad," Linus argued.

"Do you want me to help you get that surfboard or not?" Dad asserted without backing off.

"Yes," Linus replied.

"Then do it."

A few minutes later, Linus completed the task.

"So far, so good," Dad acknowledged. "You have a plan and a list of services that you can offer. Here's what you will do." Dad pointed to the client list. "We're going to type up your services so that they look professional. From this point on, every time that you meet any of the people on your client list, you will then offer them your services and let them know that you are saving to buy a surfboard by your birthday."

"That's it?" Linus questioned. "That's the whole plan?"

"Yes, indeed," Dad insisted. "We'll measure your results week by week."

Linus followed the counsel and to his surprise, almost everyone hired him to do something. Most people liked his initiative and the fact that he was working toward something specific. He even received a few extra tips.

The money began to add up and by the time he approached his birthday month, he had accumulated precisely $228.

A very proud Linus hopped in the car to drive to Ron Jon's Surf Shop and pick out his very own board–the one he earned for himself–with a helping hand from Dad.

MORAL OF THE STORY:
It's amazing what's possible when you want something badly enough and actually make a plan to achieve it.

Phase 4:
The Later Teens from 16-20.
A Time of Guiding.

"If you have a line of business–I know this as a CEO–or if you have
a teenager–I know this as a parent–who have a spending problem,
what do you do? You quit giving them money."
Carly Fiorina

Now you know their Avatar–even though they are not openly
communicating with you.

At a certain point, earlier than you would wish, their vocabulary is
reduced to single words.

QUESTION: "How was your day?"
ANSWER: "Fine."
QUESTION: "What did you do?"
ANSWER: "Nothing."

Occasionally it deteriorates even further to grunts, mumbles or
other unintelligible word-like sounds.

In this trying yet necessary time of separation and growing into
adulthood you still have an enormous opportunity to help mold your
child through one of the world's most powerful learning tools: failure.

**Failure teaches far more than success. Experimentation
and the actual process of going through the seeming agony and
embarrassment can do wonders for cementing life lessons.**

The beauty of this time period is that the failures come under a
protective umbrella, a space where, generally speaking, there is a safety net

that you provide. You can even encourage them to take calculated risks, let the leash out, allow them to go through the pain–even if they withdraw.

Avatar Keywords can act as a powerful ally. Even though your child may not respond or react, they will still hear the words that speak to their essence. You can applaud and enliven them without their realization or consent. Call it parental discretion and talk to them where they live.

Often the lines between parent and friend blur significantly–and throughout this period you are the parent first and being a friend comes second. Your help may be unwanted. Your guidance is disregarded and disdained.

Still, their name resonates as will the Keywords. The difference is that the Keywords will also influence them and build them up–and connect you, the parent, to the process.

In due course, with guidance and a few bumps and bruises, their love and openness will return. Though in a different hue, you might return to hero status after all.

SUPERPOWER STORY:
Ricky, Louie and the bug.

Ricky and Louie grew up in an entrepreneurial household. Both Mom and Dad owned multiple businesses over the years–some successful, others not–and the topic around the dining room table often revolved around strategies, challenges and new ideas.

Ricky and Louie, both brothers and best friends caught the entrepreneurial bug early. They wanted to own their own business, though happy to do so as a team. With each new concept, Mom and Dad offered counsel and support, often acting as a sounding board.

For his fifteenth birthday in August, Ricky received a windsurfing board, the only one in the entire neighborhood. By the following summer, he was ready.

"Dad–me and Louie have decided to start a windsurfing school," Ricky began. "We have the only board in the whole area and everyone wants to try it out. Since we are the only kids that know how to sail, we figure that we can teach others on our own board."

"Sounds interesting," Dad replied. "Have you thought about a license?"

"What do you mean?" Ricky asked.

"To run a school and charge money for lessons, you probably need a business license," Dad answered. "Although what I recommend is that you try out the concept first and if it catches on, then you can worry about the official paperwork."

"Good idea, Dad," Louie chimed in. "We even have a name–R&L Windsurfing."

Ricky and Louie spent most of the day at the community beach on the river, with Ricky's windsurfer in tow. For several weeks, Dad made no mention of the school. Finally, the issue surfaced at dinner.

"How's R&L Windsurfing?" Dad queried.

"Not so great," Ricky answered. "I mean it's fun and all, but nobody wants to pay us for lessons."

"Everybody keeps trying to borrow Ricky's board," Louie added. "And they all think it's weird that we want to charge them."

"And they think they can surf without a lesson." Ricky looked dejected. "I don't think this is going to work."

"Hmmm…" Dad chimed. "Maybe you ought to think of something else. You might want to survey the market first."

"What do you mean, Dad?" Ricky shot back.

"Find out if there is a need or want for your products or services before you look to make them or sell them, son. It's kind of a fundamental question in a business."

Ricky and Louie did not respond.

A few days later, they returned to their bouncy, positive selves. The bug was back.

"We have a much better idea than the sailing school," Ricky posited to both his parents. "We surveyed the market and we're going into the crabbing business."

"Tell me more," Dad said, smiling at his boys.

"Well, we asked Mr. Highsmith next door if he would buy our crabs and he told us that he would. He said he loves Maryland Blue Crabs and would pay us $3 each for up to a dozen every week for the whole rest of the summer."

Louie spoke up. "And if he will buy them, we know that other neighbors will, too."

"That's good," Dad agreed. "Have you thought about the costs?"

"What costs?" The boys voiced in unison.

"Well–I'm happy to let you use our boat, but you have to pay for the gas and the special boat oil–and to have it fixed if something breaks. I suggest you set up a reserve fund for that, just in case." Dad paused. "And what about bait and supplies?"

"We have most of what we need," Ricky said, a little miffed. "We're going to use chicken necks as bait because they are super cheap."

"It's still a cost, son, even if it's not a big one. On days when you don't catch a lot of crabs, that bait is like money down the drain. Just pay attention to your expenses–that's all. I'm not charging you for the boat–which normally would be another expense to a crabbing business."

Ricky and Louie spent the rest of the summer on the water. They caught a few crabs most days, though not enough to accumulate any money. Fortunately, Dad agreed to pay the same $3 per crab as the neighbors or they would have ended up in the red. At least they ate a lot of delicious blue crabs.

"Mom and Dad, I've decided what I can do to make some money as soon as I turn sixteen," Ricky said about a week before his birthday. "I'm going to be a babysitter. All I have to do is play with little kids and hang out until their parents come home. Then they pay me. The going rate is about $5 an hour. Awesome."

"Sounds interesting," Dad said using his standard line. "It may take more than you think."

Mom jumped in. "I can help you with this Ricky. Would you like me to make a few calls? Most of our friends and family know that you are quite responsible."

"That would be great, Mom," Ricky beamed. "I would really appreciate it."

Just after his birthday, Ricky got his first job. Aunt Jennifer hired him to watch over his two-year old cousin, Rachel, at their house. All

Ricky had to do was show up and take care of her until Aunt Jennifer and Uncle Martin came home from a dinner out.

After several successful baby-sitting evenings, Aunt Jennifer asked Ricky if he would be up for taking care of Rachel for an entire Saturday afternoon–about five hours or so. He enthusiastically agreed and took notes about what Rachel would need to eat and how she took a nap at around 2 PM.

On Saturday, Ricky showed up on time and began to play with Rachel. Right around 2 o'clock, he carried her up to her room and put her down for a nap.

As soon as Rachel fell asleep, Ricky went downstairs and began to watch TV. He vaguely remembered Aunt Jennifer saying something about how long she should sleep though figured he would hear her call out and not have to worry about it. He turned on his favorite shows.

After the fourth sitcom in a row, Ricky had a funny feeling–a weird sense that something might be wrong and that he should check on Rachel.

Up the stairs he went, down the hall and into her room to quite an alarming site.

It seems that Rachel woke herself up, took off her diaper and discovered that baby poop doubled quite well as finger paint. She proceeded to decorate her crib, the wallpaper with the fairies on it and herself in full grandeur–everything completely covered in poop.

"Oh my gosh," Ricky exclaimed, or words to that effect. "That is so disgusting. What are you doing, Rachel?"

Rachel just smiled at him. He spent the next two hours bathing her, wiping down the crib and scrubbing the wall.

Babysitting career over.

"Okay, Dad," Ricky took the lead. "I think we have a good plan for a business. We surveyed a bunch of people in the neighborhood and have determined that there is a definite need for lawn services." Ricky looked at Louie who nodded in agreement. "Many of them said that if the price was right, they will give us a chance."

"That's usually how it works, boys," Dad said as he glanced at Mom. "If you provide a good service at a better price, people will likely buy it. So what equipment do you need?"

"What do you mean?" Ricky asked.

"Don't you need at least a mower and a weed wacker–plus rakes and shovels, maybe?" Dad continued.

"Yeah, but..." Ricky stammered.

"Yeah, but, what?" Dad asked without anger or malice.

"Well we sort of figured that we'd just use our stuff," Ricky mumbled.

"That's a pretty big assumption, don't you think?" Dad said, still smiling. "If you want to start a real business, you need the proper equipment and our mower is quite old. You can use the shovels, rakes and wheelbarrow, but you'll need a new mower. Imagine what would happen if you're in the middle of cutting a lawn and your mower dies on you."

Ricky and Louie sat in silence.

"Mom and I might be willing to help fund your business, though we'd need to make a contract," Dad concluded.

"What kind of a contract?" Ricky questioned.

"One that outlines the terms of our agreement, how much money is needed, how you would pay us back and so on."

"Can you help us with that?" Ricky requested.

"Sure. We need to get down on paper what we agree to. You guys figure out how much money you need and then we'll talk about it."

Ricky and Louie went online after dinner. After about an hour they returned to discuss what they found.

"To buy a good mower and a weed wacker, we'll need just under $300," Louie presented as the spokesperson for the two. "We checked the reviews for most reliable brands."

"Okay," Dad acknowledged. "If you give me 30% of every dollar you bring in to pay for this equipment, then you'll need to make at least $1000 to return the money. You think you can do that?"

Both boys nodded their heads.

"Okay," Dad repeated. "The title to the equipment will be transferred to you once you pay off the debt. Let's get this in writing and fund this business."

For the next several months, the boys worked hard after school and on the weekends. Because their prices were so much cheaper than other professional companies, they kept busy. Unfortunately, after paying 30% back plus the cost of gas, not much was left for their own pockets.

By the time winter rolled around and they shut down for the season, they had only managed to save about $100 from all that work.

"Dad," Ricky opened with over dinner. "I think we need to raise our prices in the spring. After paying you back, we hardly made any money. If we figure in our time, we made less than a dollar an hour."

"It's not as bad as it looks, son," Dad corrected. "Because you were also buying equipment that you will own outright once paid off."

"We're barely halfway there, Dad," Ricky moaned. "It's hardly worth it. We didn't charge anywhere near enough. We might be smarter to try something else and pay you back from that."

Dad smiled at both boys. "You might want to research what others are charging and come in just a little below them. As you're suggesting, I have a feeling that you underpriced yourselves quite a bit."

"Nothing we can do now," Ricky blurted. "Season's over for the winter."

Barely a week went by before the bug returned.

"This is the one, Mom and Dad," Ricky began. "I know it is."

"We did the research on other companies doing it and got all of their pricing," Louie chimed in. "We can come in at a little less and still make a bunch of money."

"And our costs are almost zero," Ricky beamed. "It's perfect."

"And what is this new venture?" Dad asked without much expression.

"Animal services," Louie exclaimed. "Dog walking and pet sitting."

"Interesting," Dad stated.

"Our only cost is making up the brochures," Ricky disclosed.

"And we found a service online that will make them up and send them to us for $60," Louie included. "Then we go door to door and put them in everybody's mailbox.

"We have our pricing model all laid out," Ricky claimed proudly. "Check it out."

He passed a note pad across the table.

"I like it," Dad agreed. "You have low overhead, you do the work yourselves and you've created multiple streams of income. There's only one detail that you've overlooked."

"What's that?" Ricky asked.

"When you walk a dog, that money is yours. When you keep a dog at our home, that means that you create extra mess, others have to pay attention and help out when you're not here and so on. It seems to me that there should be an allowance for that in your model."

"What do you think is fair, Dad?" Ricky said as he looked over at his brother.

"25% of the pet-sitting fee," Dad responded. "And maybe until it's paid off, we can apply that against the lawn equipment." Dad glanced at Mom who nodded in agreement.

"Okay with me," Ricky said.

"Okay with me, too," Louie echoed.

Within two weeks Ricky and Louie had three dog clients. Over the next few months they picked up several more and when pet sitting, learned how to make money while they slept.

Even though they paid off the equipment, they never did go back to cutting lawns.

While many might consider Ricky and Louie's first ventures as failures, Mom and Dad didn't view them that way–or at the very least, the boys failed their way into success.

From the windsurfing school they learned about surveying the market.

From crabbing, they found out about costs.

From babysitting, Ricky had his first encounter with unacceptable risk.

From lawn services, they grasped the value of research and proper pricing.

With the animal care business, they found their niche and continued earning good spending money all the way until college.

MORAL OF THE STORY:
In the words of First Lady Eleanor Roosevelt: "Children are likely to live up to what you believe of them." Let's let them try, fall down, make mistakes and fail their way forward.

Sibling Spending Discrepancies

"To understand someone, find out how he spends his money."
~ Mason Cooley

So why do families have siblings that run the gamut when it comes to monetary responsibility even when raised in the same household?

Why is one sibling loaded with credit card debt as an adult and the other only makes purchases on a debit card? Most parents try to treat their children equally and raise them in the same way. Why does one live paycheck to paycheck and drive a Lexus while the other is overloaded with cash reserves and drives a used Ford with 150 thousand miles on its odometer?

Why does one donate money to charities while the other gives little to nothing? Yes, many extenuating factors apply such as your chosen trade, career, salary, college loans, and others–though generally, siblings start out with equal financial opportunities. What they don't start out with is the same Avatar nor the same interpretation of money.

Money is nothing more than a means to exchange goods. Kids trade Halloween candy, sports cards, actions figures, and even food in the lunchroom with their classmates. Money is tied to emotions and desires for kids (and adults, for that matter, on a more complex level).

As the value of a dollar is being developed, the parent has the biggest influence in shaping the child's understanding and respect for it.

Teaching money responsibility begins with family values and memorializing beliefs through words, actions and shared experiences. These lay the groundwork so that kids better learn to

ethically navigate decisions as they grow. **How our children apply the family values we teach will be different to how we applied them. We must embrace and pay attention to those differences.**

Children live out family values given the tools and parameters with which they operate and communicate–including social media and their devices. These directly impact their view of the world and their understanding of money.

So how can children develop a sense of accomplishment and self worth?

What happens when they go to buy something with their own money? What do they learn when they don't have enough and ask you for help? Do they understand the notion of borrowing from their next allowance? Do they grasp at a young age that if they "borrow" it will be deducted later?

As children age, the complexities compound.

Do they know how to tie out credits and debits?

Can they reconcile a bank statement or a monthly credit card print out?

Assuming they conceptually know the mechanics, do they understand spending parameters and what is appropriate in a given situation?

If they receive a gift card, do they look to spend it down to the penny, or acquire only what they need in the moment and save the rest?

When they earn and spend their own money, they gradually gain a better sense of how it works–a learning process that carries on into adulthood.

As Dr. Seuss once quoted: "Adults are just outdated children."

SUMMARY:

- A child's Avatar forms organically, one filament of belief at a time.
- Your behavior as a parent has an enormous influence on the Avatar formation of your children.
- Children have difficulty or prove resistant to expressing their Avatar.
- Even when children resist communicating, you can still reach them through Avatar Keywords.

CALL TO ACTION:

Determine the Avatars of your children. Use Avatar Keywords in your communication in order to reach them at their essence.

Chapter 7

HOW DO YOUR PARENTS HANDLE MONEY?

Do they live in abundance or are they stuck in the Great Depression?

"Risk comes from not knowing what you're doing."
~ Warren Buffett

Count on change.

The one thing we can absolutely count on without fail is change. It is guaranteed, year in and year out. As we age, this gives rise to a challenging dilemma. Most elders become more and more resistant to change on all levels, including financial matters. Whether we like it or not, market conditions shift constantly. Tax and regulatory codes change on an annual basis, giving rise to new conditions. Politics influence all aspects of finances. Therefore, it is virtually impossible that the same plan that worked well ten or even five years ago will work the same way today.

A 2014 Fidelity report said that over 60% percent of adult parents over age 55 are more comfortable discussing issues with their advisors than with their adult children over 30. This points to a marked absence of trust–often with good reason. An understanding of each others' Avatars can at the very least help with communication issues.

While essential that parents seek objective advice about their finances, generally from other than their own adult children, the need for their children's involvement should never be overlooked. The upcoming transfer of wealth by baby boomers poses emotional stress for both sides–parents and children–and not everyone is qualified for the role that they find themselves in due to circumstance, often unexpectedly.

The best course of action is for parents to involve children in planning and decision making along with certified financial professionals. This ensures that everyone gets on the same page, brings awareness to the wishes of parents and establishes a clear path to accomplishing them.

If the professional has a keen understanding of Emotional Intelligence, he or she can serve to bridge the gap, openly discuss differing points of views and provide better guidance for all.

Without question, poor planning or a failure to make plans can lead to disastrous consequences.

KRYPTONITE STORY:
No business with minors.

A new client came to us after deciding to move back to their state of origin. They wanted to sell their house in Scottsdale, Arizona and return to the Pacific Northwest. We reviewed their assets and came across the deed to the Scottsdale home–a sizeable mansion worth well over seven figures. "Who are these other three people on the deed?" we asked them. "Oh, those are our grandchildren. We included them on the deed when we bought the house so that we can save on inheritance taxes later." "How old are they?" we questioned. "Eight, ten and eleven at this point," our client answered. "We gave them each an equal share."

"How did you find out about the inheritance tax issue?" we pushed.

"Oh, we learned about it from a friend. Our house has gone up in value by almost double and we didn't want the government to get all of our money."

"Was your friend a lawyer?" we inquired.

"No–just a savvy investor that we respect. He made a lot of money in real estate."

We sat in the meeting wondering how to best communicate the nightmare they created. "Well, we have some bad news," we began. "Your friend may have been a smart investor, though he knew very little about minors. A minor cannot control any real estate and cannot sign any documents. Their parents in this case, who may be in a conflict of interest, cannot act on their behalf. This means that every individual grandchild would need a legal guardian who acts for them and protects their interest. First the guardians would need to approve the sale of the house. Then they would need to approve your purchase of a new house as being in the best interests of the grandchildren. If the house you purchase is lesser in value than your home in Scottsdale, then the difference would need to be placed in trust for your grandchildren."

"Is there anything at all we can do?" they asked, dumbfounded.

"Sure," we replied. "You can wait until they are all eighteen and hope that they agree with your decision. At that point, they will own 60% of the house."

MORAL OF THE STORY:
When you need a plumber, don't call an electrician.

That dreaded technology.

"There are some problems that technology can't solve."
~ Nick Bostrom

Many older adults feel flat out terrified of technology. Often, they shun it or avoid it like the plague. As it keeps changing at ever increasing speeds this gives rise to even greater challenges. What worked yesterday no longer works. What works today will be obsolete in short order. It's no wonder many fear it or at least feel uncomfortable.

In the financial realm, Robo Advisors are disrupting the industry, with do-it-yourselfers finding an ill-found sense of independence. Many of them actually believe that an online program can replace the human experience.

Financial advisors understand that technology can't replace the capability of the human mind, only enhance it.

The insights provided by knowing someone's Kryptonite allow that human touch to come alive and forge a deeper bond than can ever be achieved with technology alone.

The financial advisor commands more responsibility than ever in today's economy–including the efficient and proper use of technology to provide answers. Software helps the competent and good advisors in our industry to wash out the poor and unequipped advisors who don't deliver enough value. In an ideal scenario, technology frees up the advisor and enables them to spend more time with the client, assuaging their fears and focusing on the human element. Superpowers can be maximized. Kryptonites can be met with understanding and gentility as opposed to a dispassionate computer-generated response. This applies more than anywhere with parents and elders who require and stand to benefit the most from the extra touch.

KRYPTONITE STORY:
I'm sticking with Solitaire...

"It only takes a few clicks, Mom," Leonard said to his mother who called herself "Kayla" which allegedly meant "grandmother" in some obscure language. She had ten grandkids and could call herself whatever she wanted.

"I tried that," Kayla countered. "It didn't work. It didn't do anything."

Leonard paused for a moment. "You have to turn on the browser, Mom," he blurted out.

"What's a browser?" she asked.

"It's the thing that gets you from website to website."

"Oh," Kayla replied. "I thought the internet did that."

Leonard paused again. "Yes, of course," he agreed. "But it's kind of like this. Think of the internet as a big city. In the city there are websites, like buildings that contain things. You have shopping websites that act just like stores, service websites that are like businesses and you have to move from one to another to get what you need. The browser does that for you, kind of like taking a taxi on the internet."

"Oh," Kayla sighed, still perplexed. She did her best to appear like she understood.

Leonard raised his index finger. "You have to use a browser to get from place to place and you have to log in, kind of like calling a taxi to get a ride."

He watched her face go blank.

"I have an idea," he began, after a long pause. "We'll just leave the browser on the whole time and you'll never have to worry about it."

He sat back, pleased with himself.

"I don't want to do that," Kayla objected.

"Why not?"

"I heard from my friends that it's dangerous–kind of like the microwave. If you stand in front of it while it's on, it sort of fries your brain a little. I always turn my computer off when I finish with it."

"Mom," Leonard pursed his lips. "That's just not true. The only problem with leaving your computer on is that it leaves it more susceptible to picking up a virus. That's all."

"Well that's terrible!" Kayla exclaimed. "The last thing we need around here is a virus. Do you know how hard I work to keep your father healthy? Do you realize that he's a borderline diabetic?"

Leonard threw up his hands. "No, Mom–not that kind of virus. It's a computer virus, only on the internet."

"I don't care," Kayla jabbered. "I don't want any kind of virus around here. People pass those back and forth in this nursing home all the time. Do you have any idea how hard it is to keep your father away from sweets? His blood sugar can spike in a heartbeat. I've taken him to the hospital multiple times."

"Mom," Leonard emitted, a mix of frustration and resignation. "So what do you want to do?"

She looked at him softly and put her wrinkled palm on his neck. "You take care of our computer stuff, Len. You're good at this. I'm going to stick to my Solitaire."

MORAL OF THE STORY:
You can lead a horse to water, but you can't ever make him drink.

Are we still fighting World War II?

OLD
THINKING

"Man is still the most extraordinary computer of all."
~ John F. Kennedy

Ask the wrong questions and you are guaranteed to get the wrong answers.

Can you finally retire?

Do you have enough money?

What happens on that date when you walk out of your office for the last time, ready for the sunset on your sailboat, extended cruises in the Caribbean and wine tours in Napa during the harvest?

Are those dreams still possible or nothing more than pie-in-the-sky?

Mainstream advertising paints a picture of a rosy new life that happens almost automatically when you reach that long awaited retirement date.

Does it ever play out that way?

Are you doing enough to provide for later–particularly if you want to maintain your lifestyle?

We've all heard the adage that leopards don't change their spots. Regrettably, the further we age, the difficulty in making any change increases. With this in mind, the alternative of understanding our Avatars and consequent Superpowers and Kryptonites becomes ever more critical. If we know that change is unlikely or at least very challenging, it becomes far more effective to adapt, not alter, to enhance strengths and account for weaknesses, instead of making hard turns into new directions.

Hopefully as we age and gain experience, we work a little less and make a little more–which enables a more aggressive saving and investing plan. Periodic reviews and adapting to change will optimize growth and open the door for a retirement with options.

Only a proactive and integrated tax and investment plan with a unified team of advisors that understands you and works within your view of the world will ensure that you can live your vision through the golden years.

Trying to do it all yourself is a guaranteed formula for failure.

KRYPTONITE STORY:
No pain, no gain.

Jack and Debbie worked with their investment advisor for years. When the advisor retired they needed someone new quarterbacking their financial picture.

Their advisor's successor was quite a bit younger and recommended an overhaul to their portfolio with new technology they did not understand. Interviews with a handful of other firms brought on only more confusion.

Throughout their search, they consistently heard that their portfolio was outdated with investments that failed to address current market challenges. Their portfolio was criticized for not having individual stocks or bonds, for an excess of overlapping investment strategies and for poor technology that failed to track their performance. They were told that they carried high management expenses, had weak short term performance and a handful of other items that made them feel uneasy.

They knew adjustments were needed, but found it difficult to grasp the right course of action.

Jack and Debbie invited their adult children over for Sunday dinner and the topic of finances came up. Their youngest, Aaron, was 26 and stated that no one needed financial advisors in these times because technology was so advanced. He had all his funds with a Robo Advisor so he could "set it and forget it." All he had to do was fill out an investor questionnaire and his portfolio was complete. He didn't need to talk to anyone because an algorithm would handle his needs.

Millie, their middle child disagreed with him and chose a different route. She saved everything into her work retirement plan and placed some money with a discount broker. She would call every now and then to get advice from a live person.

Everyone agreed that a change needed to be made by the parents, though the family came to a standstill. They recognized that their retired advisor had not kept up with the times, but felt nervous about overhauling their portfolio with someone new or using a computer based software. What about a good ol' face-to-face meeting to discuss their financial needs? Didn't that count for something anymore? After all, they would need to start drawing income soon and had far more complex investment issues than their children.

Though they knew that both children took action that made sense to them, they couldn't determine the correct balance for their own situation. Overwhelmed and exhausted, Jack and Debbie did nothing and hoped for the best.

MORAL OF THE STORY:
If you only hope for the best, prayer may be your best option.

SUMMARY:

- Change is inevitable though far more difficult for aging parents, regardless of their Avatars.
- Technology only makes life easier if understood and embraced.
- To amass wealth, or even a nest egg large enough for retirement, a team of professionals is an absolute mandate.

CALL TO ACTION:

Review your current team. What changes do you need to make? Who needs to be added? Does everyone in your family understand your goals and objectives? Do they know each others' Avatars? Are they working together to achieve those goals using each others' Superpowers?

Chapter 8

ARE YOU AFRAID OF THE MAN?

Uncle Sam giveth and so quickly he taketh away. Those dreaded taxes– YES, they can wipe you out.

"In this world, the only thing that is certain is death and taxes."
~ Benjamin Franklin

We all face the same ugly bottom line: like it or not, we must pay taxes.

We drive on roads. We rely on police and military for safety. We require infrastructure to survive.

Do we believe that the government is a better steward of our money than we would be? No, not at all. Except that it doesn't matter what you believe. You pay or you suffer–eventually. As the government systems improve at auditing, more violators will get caught.

So what's the solution?

Understand clearly what you can write off and play to your strengths (your Superpower). Uncle Sam allows us to take hundreds of deductions and as long as you follow the rules, there is nothing wrong with being opportunistic and not giving "The Man" a penny more than he deserves.

All of us excel at certain things, yet not all things. When it comes to taxes, the code changes all the time and unless you're a full time tax practitioner, you'll likely fall behind the newest revisions, make mistakes or pay more than you should. The government doesn't care how much you know or don't know. They don't care when you make a mistake in their favor. They care a lot when you make a mistake that favors you.

KRYPTONITE STORY:

It ain't never "on the side..."

Jim Benson had a solid position at a large corporation as an IT manager. He ran a small team charged with keeping company computer systems running and did such a good job that he seldom worked extra hours and had a fair amount of time on his hands.

"Why not moonlight a little?" he thought to himself. Several of the executives from a number of clients often expressed a personal need for IT help and he never had anyone to refer them to–until he thought of himself.

"I already pay my taxes," he reflected, since they came out of every paycheck. "Why not make a little extra on the side?"

He began to offer his talents out to hire, picking up a few clients who always paid "in full." What a joy! No extra deductions.

That added money came in handy–financed the down payment on a jet-ski and a white water rafting trip as well as a few nice dinners along the way. It never occurred to Jim that those executives would actually declare him as an expense.

For three years he took care of a select group of clients on a sporadic basis, though they all seemed to come back to him again and again with various needs.

Then came the notice from the IRS. He was being audited.

Apparently a cross check of the expenses of a certain client didn't reflect a corresponding reported income by Jim.

As the auditor dug deeper, Jim's other clients surfaced, all of them having reported Jim as an expense.

Except it never occurred to Jim to declare them as income.

Oops!

MORAL OF THE STORY:
In the words of Albert Einstein: "The hardest thing in the world to understand is the income tax."

The Lord giveth and the Man taketh away.

"What is the difference between a taxidermist and a tax collector?
The taxidermist takes only your skin."
~ Mark Twain

Why do 99% of Americans overpay in taxes and allow their Kryptonite to take over?

No one likes to pay money to Uncle Sam that is rightfully theirs.

Most often, the real answer is because the overwhelming majority of us are focused on succeeding at our job, raising children and participating in hobbies and interests after work and on weekends.

In other words, 99% of Americans have no system.

It's easier to ignore your tax situation and "hope for the best." This often creates a subconscious doubt or fear that the IRS is going to take more money than you think is fair and causes analysis paralysis in planning for yourself and your business.

It can also give rise to irrational decision making as you contemplate paying taxes–a condition that can be exacerbated by your Kryptonite. Before you know it, the deadline looms before you and you hope the number from your tax expert comes in below a subjective figure you created in your head, despite the little knowledge you have of the tax code and how it relates to the dollars you owe.

When you understand when and how to pay taxes you gain clarity.

Even more importantly, you gain knowledge and power to be forward thinking and can plan how to reduce your tax liability when financially impacting life events take place.

Contrast that with the subconscious worry and uncertainty that you may be faced with paying an unknown amount. This includes job changes, children, marriage, divorce, starting a business, selling your home, making a large investment and so on.

The Wealthy Avatar that you will learn about in the next chapter focuses on both–the day to day path to financial independence and the extraordinary implications of dealing with any significant life event.

The mundane daily grind must be set on "an autopilot to success" while each major turn in the road needs careful planning and consideration, particularly with respect to taxes.

KRYPTONITE STORY:
To go or not to go...

Armando's company tapped him on the shoulder at work. "We'd like you to relocate to Phoenix. It will, of course, involve a substantial promotion."

Armando's heart sank. He knew he would go nowhere in the company unless he accepted and yet, what would his wife, Lesley, do? What happened to her job? What about their two kids and their education? How would they know what school district to move into? What about the grandparents who lived nearby? So many questions.

With a heavy heart, Armando shared the news with his wife.

Lesley immediately felt trapped. Was this even the right thing for their marriage? What about taxes? Even the relocation and moving allowance was taxable. What about the sale of their home? They'd have to pay taxes on that–and they didn't even know if they should buy another one or take their furniture with them. She knew they would lose money if they sold it–that's for sure.

And wait–even though Armando's salary went up, what if she couldn't find a job? It's not as if his wage increase would totally make up for the loss of hers. If she did find a job, her income plus that of her husband could push them into a higher tax bracket. Then what?

Not only that, without grandparents nearby, they'd have to pay for childcare. Not much of this made sense and it put a serious wrench into their relationship. Maybe they should just forget the whole idea and stay where they are.

MORAL OF THE STORY:
Learn the rules—if you ignore them, the government will assume that you would rather give them your money than preserve it for your spouse and children.

Understand the pieces.

"As American taxpayers know too well, the tax code is
incredibly complex and compliance is all too expensive."
~ Jim Ramstad

There are two main components to taxes, income and deductions. **Your income is where you have the ability to make the most impact. You control your level of focus on your job, your performance and the consequent benefits of your labor.**

By contrast, your deductions are more elusive and require careful attention.

Being knowledgeable and proactive about your deductions is different than creating deductions simply to reduce your tax liability.

It's better to earn a dollar and pay 25 cents in taxes than to spend 1 dollar only to save 25 cents in taxes. If you spend 1 dollar to avoid paying taxes, then you essentially spend 75 cents to save 25 cents. That 75 cents can certainly be put to better use.

If your local department store has a 50% off sale on shoes, that doesn't mean you save money if you buy them. You only save money if you actually need a new pair of shoes. If not, it's simply another expense.

That's not to say you shouldn't seek out how to maximize your deductions through everyday activities.

When you understand which deductions appropriately apply, you ensure that you take all that are available.

Then what are these deductions and how are they generally broken down?

Your personal tax return contains schedules. The main ones are Schedules A through E on your 1040 or personal tax return. They form the core sections that determine the tax you owe or the refund you are due from the government. Here is a breakdown:

Schedule A

You can either elect to take a standard deduction or itemize your deductions. If your itemized deductions exceed the standard deduction, then it typically makes sense to itemize.

Itemized deductions include your mortgage interest, charitable contributions, work related expenses, state taxes, and so on.

If you aren't aware of these deductions, then you put yourself at a disadvantage when it comes time to submit your tax information to your preparer. Other than the standard forms that are mailed to you as required by law, no one will track or tell you which work related expenses can reduce your tax liability.

95% of Americans "guesstimate" their work related expenses. Most people erroneously report these deductions by understating the expenses because they don't track them properly throughout the year.

"Guesstimating" hurts you in two ways. You either overpay for failure to account properly for all of your expenses or you put yourself at risk if audited by the IRS because you claim more than you deserve.

 Kryptonite Danger: Claiming the wrong amount of charitable deductions due to lack of tracking–you either pay too much because of lack of knowledge or you pay too little and the Man comes knocking.

SOLUTION: Create a simple tracking system and train yourself to record every expense. Develop this one crucial habit. When it comes to charities, decide what organizations are most important to you at the beginning of the year and how much you intend to contribute. If you want to be more generous at the end of the year and add additional charities or contribute a larger amount, then do it all at once and document it clearly.

Schedule B

This lists the income you receive via dividends and or interest payments. Documentation of interest and dividends are usually provided to you by a company that holds your investments. However, in many situations such as private loans or closely held corporations it isn't that simple. You are required to pay a certain tax rate on interest and dividends. If you have a ballpark figure as to how much you will receive throughout the year, you can accurately gauge how much you will owe at the end of the year and avoid surprises.

 Kryptonite Danger: Forgetting to report accounts with 1099 income thus triggering IRS inquiries–a visit you are never happy to receive.

SOLUTION: Cross check prior year returns for any accounts you may have missed. If you move or change addresses, then triple check for any accounts that may have slipped through the cracks.

Schedule C

This reports the income or loss for a business that acts as a sole proprietor. Most taxpayers inaccurately report their expenses on this form because they do not have a process to track what expenses they incur and can deduct. Know what categories apply to you. For example, most people don't accurately report home office expenses.

Even a "shoebox" method as an approach is better than nothing. Every time you incur an expense, throw the receipts in a "shoebox." Alternatively, scan the receipts into an app on your smartphone.

You now have a centralized location that you can return to and tally up the appropriate expenses in the correct category. Throwing them in a shoebox will serve you better than having to locate, review, and comb through your bank or credit cards statements for hours upon end.

When you pay cash to park for a business meeting, do you keep the receipt? If not, then how likely is it for you to remember every single expense over 365 days?

Kryptonite Danger: Overlooking tax deductions for expenses paid on a personal credit card–do you really want to pay more than you're supposed to?

SOLUTION: Get a separate business credit or debit card and review your year end personal statements as a back-up precautionary measure.

Schedule D

If you sell an asset, then the gain or loss must be reported on Schedule D. Did you sell stocks, a piece of property, your home, or even a car?

These sales are broken down into Short Term and Long Term Gains and Losses that can offset each other.

You must also record each transaction when you acquire an asset to take advantage of deductions or capital expenditures as you own and depreciate or improve it. Note that the sale of that asset could be years down the road. If you buy a piece of property, many items need to be tracked along the way. For example, if you renovate a kitchen or buy a new HVAC you must record the actual cost basis–what you payed for it.

Clients scramble frequently over assets they bought years ago and neglected to track expenses. When they can't locate the receipts, they lose the deductions, plain and simple.

There may even be expenses when you acquire an asset that can translate to your Schedule A deductions. **Various schedules potentially affect each other and a lack of awareness will cause you to pay unnecessary tax.**

 Kryptonite Danger: Reporting the incorrect cost after a stock is sold.

SOLUTION: Pay attention to the details at the beginning because Uncle Sam won't do it for you.

Schedule E

You can report income or losses from S-Corporations, rental real estate, royalties, trusts, estates, partnerships, and others. This section tends to get far more complicated and the use of a professional is highly recommended.

 Kryptonite Danger: Filing your tax return too early before getting all your K-1's. Return amendments by your tax preparer cost money that you'll never get back.

SOLUTION: Patience! Uncle Sam never rewards you for filing early.

 ## KRYPTONITE STORY:
Leave it to the Welsh.

Jason and Mary Kineash had no biological kids but a lot of "childlike" expenses. They rationalized that the clothing, bedding, toys, doctor bills and food for their four Welsh Corgis were no different than other parents' who claimed allowable deductions for their children. Jason decided to list them all as dependents—Wesley, Ferdinand, Rip and Dylan. They might even have gotten away with it except that the word "dog" in front of "food" in their deductions spilled the beans.

MORAL OF THE STORY:
Dogs may be man's best friend, but they are not deductible.

SUMMARY:

- No one can avoid paying taxes–at least not if you actually make money.
- If you fail to track and record allowable deductions you will overpay and give the government part of your hard earned income.
- If you underpay it will only be temporary. Unwanted friends will show up with their hands extended and the number you end up paying will increase due to penalties.
- Unless you are a trained tax professional, pay the freight to hire one.
- WARNING: Pay close attention to your Kryptonite. Don't let it subconsciously blind you with respect to addressing your tax needs–a mistake that can hound you for years.

CALL TO ACTION:

Review your current tracking and recording system. Do you use software or an app? How do you communicate with your tax preparer? What systems do you have in place to capture all deductions?

Chapter 9

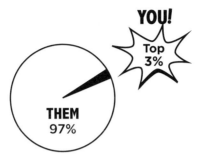

BECOME A
WEALTHY AVATAR

The quickest path by far is to convert your Kryptonite into your greatest ally!

"If investing is entertaining, if you're having fun, you're probably not making any money. Good investing is boring."
~ George Soros

We come into this world as a blank slate.

Right, wrong or otherwise, the slate fills up quickly with ideas, prejudices, viewpoints and perspectives tainted by the experience of those who lived them before us. We cannot avoid this.

Our very survival depends on figuring out at a base level the most common and efficient way of going from a state of need or desire to a state of satisfaction–the sense that all is well in the world. This defines your belief system that in turn creates your Avatar.

Regrettably, this necessary process in no way guarantees monetary success nor financial longevity. It doesn't matter what your origin, background, bloodline or last name–you have no assurance that you will become wealthy or maintain any level of wealth.

Story upon story prove that even those in the most privileged of circumstance tumble from the pinnacle to the wasteland in record time and in a dazzling array of fashions.

The one sure-fire way to increase your own odds of financial success is to emulate those who came before you, then educate yourself as to their practices and find ways to implement those over a sustained period of time.

Because our individual Avatars determine how we view the world– how we think, speak and act–they influence everything, including our relationship with money. What they will never do is predict our financial success. They simply show us our strength in the form of our Superpower and our weakness in the form of our Kryptonite.

The Wealthy Avatar understands that on an organic level, the most direct and secure path to lasting wealth lies in overcoming your Kryptonite and turning it into your subtle advantage.

Since it will undoubtedly influence you and guide every aspect of your behavior, why not do what others never consider? Make it your friend and ally, that quiet driver that shapes your destiny. Think about it. For each of the seven Avatars, consider the **Average Avatar.**

 **Over-Commitment**   The Average Giver's Kryptonite is Over-Commitment. You say "yes" to too many things and overload your plate with tasks, many of which are insignificant, at least from a financial perspective.

A full plate leads to mistakes, stress, and a failure to focus on where true leverage points exist–those that drive you to the greatest value contributions. Too many Givers end up tired, strained and in constant "fire-fighting" mode, chasing one crisis after another.

By contrast, the Wealthy Giver understands the power of generosity and believes that the Law of Reciprocity applies at all times–particularly when well-managed.

When you give, much comes back to you and therefore much attention should be paid to the recipients and the causes you choose to support. Over-Commitment gives way to discernment and an understanding that if you place your effort in small causes, you leave little energy in the tank for those that make a far greater impact. From a financial perspective, the world seldom rewards intention. Only results matter. To the degree that your efforts remain targeted on areas where you provision high levels of value, you in turn receive your due reward. The Wealthy Givers develop the habit of deflecting requests so that you create space to consider whether each "ask" leverages your time and value at the highest level. Do not allow others to take you off course. It's all about focus and surrounding yourself with allies that keep you on track.

 **The Average Connector's Kryptonite is Waste.** So much time and effort goes into making everyone like you or at least trust you.

How many of those "connections" are centered on those that care little about you or certainly contribute virtually nothing to your financial success? How many hours go into doing "one more thing" for someone who doesn't even realize that you are the object of their attention, wrapped up in their own foibles and challenges? What if you focused all of that effort on those bonds and relationships that supported your financial success and took you to another level?

By contrast, the Wealthy Connector understands the immense power of the right connections, those that propel you forward. You know that a certain code of integrity drives those at the highest levels of success and that this code must become ingrained into the fiber of your being for them to include you.

You recognize that a single relationship can mark the difference between bumbling along and soaring to heights unimagined by most. You focus not on pleasing everyone but rather on seeking out those like-minded AND successful individuals who want to make a difference in the world in a connected way.

The Wealthy Connector bonds with those who execute on their promise to forge a meaningful relationship and discards those who in any way jeopardize the relationship or the trust it creates.

Paralysis The Average Problem Solver's Kryptonite is **Paralysis.** Despite your expertise in coming up with solutions, it is so easy for you to get stuck in the trees and miss the forest completely.

The quick fix in the moment in no way determines the overall trajectory of the whole. It is simply one small piece in a much larger picture that if ignored or misunderstood keeps you on a treadmill that never stops churning while you wonder where it ends. And then suddenly, you find yourself stuck in a rut, paralyzed, staring at the canvas of your life speculating as to your lack of results despite your unique ability to problem solve.

The Wealthy Problem Solver understands with the fabric of their character that the greatest solutions stem from a team effort. You grasp that the collective brain trust will, by definition, be far more powerful than your own private reasoning abilities, however cognitive, judicious or level-headed they may be.

You reach out for solutions from experts, listen and take in advice, follow proven paths that help you avoid playing small. It makes more sense to seek aid and counsel than to try to figure out everything on your own, particularly when it comes to the complex world of finance. Having a trusted group of experts support you as you challenge each problem, solve it, and champion the process on a larger scale brings you self-gratification. You relish knowing that a larger group participated in the ultimate outcome that benefits the collective even more.

 **Change** The Average Innovator's Kryptonite is Change and the constant yearning to tweak, adjust and initiate pulls focus from proven methods that work–even if not your own.

Your desire to learn by association fuels your need to insert new impressions into current systems and processes, regardless of their fit or lack thereof. Your quest for bigger, better, faster may build a bulkhead that showcases avant-garde approaches though seldom translates into financial gain. It's simply unique and inventive. Investing and growing economic muscle is largely formulaic and boring—the antithesis of what you stand for.

The Wealthy Innovator both comprehends and appreciates that innate in the concept of change is the search for superior knowledge, sharper saws and best-of-breed investors that can point you in a more effective and efficient way to wealth.

You welcome the idea of surrounding yourself with those highly capable in the complexities of commerce and learning what improvements they make to the norm. It's a better way to wealth and you understand that fully.

The Wealthy Innovator knows when to champion change quickly and when it creates imbalance—and makes the choice to either drive forward or step aside according to the circumstance—in either case a decision based in full personal power.

 **The Average Perfectionist's Kryptonite is Rigidity.** A lack of innate creativity stifles your ability to see opportunities outside of a tightly defined space and by definition closes you down from alternatives that don't fit your paradigm.

You fall into the trap of "same ol', same ol'" and remain closed off from new influences and directions. If the path seems unclear or unpredictable, seldom will you venture down it, choosing instead to remain in the comfort of your controlled space.

The Wealthy Perfectionist understands that systems do in fact produce foreseeable and calculable results, particularly if established by a variety of Avatars with different and unique capabilities.

You resonate with and yearn for systems without the need to be the creator of them, choosing instead to follow those proven to have succeeded at the highest level. Collaboration becomes key to your success and as long as the path to wealth is understood, you embrace it and support it wholeheartedly. The system comes from your team, not just you. The Wealthy Perfectionist holds strong to proven systems and allows tweaks to make the system better. Even when mistakes are made, corrections lead to improvements and the strength of a trusted advisory group will ultimately create better systems, drive predictable outcomes and yield growing levels of success.

 **Isolation**   **The Average Rebel's Kryptonite is Isolation.** In a world driven simultaneously by collaboration and specialization, survival on a self-created island leaves little room for teamwork, support and alliances–and yet only meager accomplishments happen without these key elements.

Even with a driving force of challenging convention, when you find alternatives, what can you do with them in the absence of a team or a network that buys into your ideas? There is no road to riches in segregation or reclusion.

The Wealthy Rebel espouses the idea of challenging the system within the system. It is perfectly fitting and warranted to act as a differentiating voice within the parameters of proven principles in triumphant circles.

You will not isolate yourself when you voice your distinctive perspective to those curious to learn from it and take their own game to a superior level. In turn, they will guide you and offer you unique ways that suit your personality and assist you to achieve success at the highest levels.

The Wealthy Rebel questions old and antiquated ideas, not the actual people who put them forward and in turn causes many to challenge their thinking and change their own status quo–a win-win for all sides.

Complexity   The Average Master's Kryptonite is **Complexity.** Despite the desire and ability to take most any issue to another level, the fascination for the convoluted and circuitous marks a death knell for the straightforward, dull path to financial ascendancy.

The systems for accumulating wealth may seem routine, drab and lackluster, yet the benefits in terms of freedom and derivable options open up the world to you. You can take it as far as your heart desires, if and only if, you keep it simple. Otherwise, complexity will bog you down, keep you mired in details and distracted or unobservant to the purity of a highly effective spartan path.

The Wealthy Master respects not only his own superior knowledge, but that of others that he associates with. You accept and practice that often times using simplicity in your communication with others can not only infer a deeper level of understanding, but bring to light the importance of having it.

You seek out those who have walked the road to success before you, admire and luxuriate in their wisdom and foresight, appreciate that you, too, can learn so much from them—as well as benefit from the trail they forged to date.

The tendency to over-complicate things is sublimated to the desire for real results that provide you with ever greater freedom to acquire knowledge. When you merge your powerful proficiency with proven pathways, there is nothing that can stop you. Those who paved the way to financial success vindicate that which you already know, as long as you get out of your own way.

Average Avatars fall prey to their Kryptonite, often without even knowing it.

Wealthy Avatars take concrete, deliberate and conscious steps to understand and overcome their Kryptonite.

They convert their Kryptonite into a geiger that measures their success, into an ally that drives them—which further highlights the difference between the Average Avatar and the Wealthy Avatar.

The Average Avatar simply exists and even with increased awareness, takes little initiative to move their financial needle. The Wealthy Avatar takes their improved awareness and puts it into action immediately.

The Wealthy Avatar understands two pivotal and undeniable axioms about wealth accumulation.

First, you can't do it alone. You need an irrefutable, circumstantiated and validated team that supports you with solid planning, investment guidance, and tax advice.

Second, you must use proven systems for success—tried and true, tested methods that work and are constantly updated and improved upon by your team. You want simple. Clean. Even boring. Yet effective and direct pathways to financial freedom.

We call it the Wealthy Avatar Journey.

The Wealthy Avatar Journey

There are six step-by-step stages to becoming a Wealthy Avatar.

STAGE 1

Discover Your Avatar

"The two most important days in your life are
the day you are born and the day you find out why."
~ Mark Twain

STAGE 1 involves a process of self-discovery and awareness that carries immediate benefits. You become reintroduced to yourself at a more pure level. You understand WHY you do what you do in thoughts, words and deeds. You learn about your driving strength, your Superpower and your prevailing weakness, your Kryptonite.

You begin to understand your relationship with money based on your Avatar—and how at your core, your beliefs surrounding money have a profound influence on your financial decision-making which dictate your current level of success.

It is eye-opening and electrifying. You, perhaps for the first time, understand YOU. Embrace the sense of inner-peace derived from this once-in-a-lifetime experience.

Build your Emotional Intelligence

"Alone we can do so little. Together we can do so much."
~ Helen Keller

You begin STAGE 2 by learning about the other Avatars. What do they stand for and believe in? How do you interact with each one? More importantly, how do your Kryptonites collide to cause relational damage and what can you do to turn that around? You start to understand how to unite and maximize your Superpower with the Superpowers of those around you, including:

- Your colleagues or team members at work.
- Your spouse or life partner.
- Your children.
- Your parents.
- Anyone close to you.

Your ability to influence those in your sphere will increase dramatically, as will your understanding of how they think and view the world. You can begin to apply the concept "Read their Mind and Connect with their Heart" through your knowledge and understanding of their Avatars. Your communication, especially about money, will become more productive and collaborative and much less dictatorial or one-sided because you will "see" through their eyes (their Avatar) as well as your own. This a selfless stage and a critical STAGE to building the mindset for teamwork that is required at the highest levels of financial success.

Build your Financial Intelligence.

"Success is doing what you want, when you want, where you want, with whom you want, as much as you want."
~ Tony Robbins

In STAGE 3 you assemble your financial toolbox. You refine the process of goal setting. You establish an accountability and review schedule for all aspects of your professional life. This is the time to initiate long-term planning and a broadening of your perspective to include the path to the old school term of "retirement" or what you now know as the financial freedom to live on your terms. The act of looking forward through objective eyes will reveal the flaws in your current procedures and strategies (assuming you have them).

You will start to grasp the art of self-correction and the absolute mandate to divorce your thinking from the herd that follows uninformed friends, colleagues or pundits in favor of a straightforward and proven process of goal setting, measuring, re-assessing, adjusting and moving forward intelligently without any influence from rash or knee-jerk reactions. This become crucial to your success over time and the building of a foundation that only gets stronger as well as the walls and the moats that protect your financial castle.

Build your Tax Intelligence.

"And I have to point out that government doesn't tax to get the money it needs, government always needs the money it gets."
~ Ronald Reagan

In STAGE 4 you secure a basic understanding of how taxes truly work and in particular how they affect your financial picture. At the end of the day, you will always be the de facto Chief Financial Officer of your finances. This does not mean that you do all the work. Quite the opposite. You establish the goals and objectives to be achieved and you then delegate the responsibility of effectively managing and controlling the taxation aspects to experts who support you–in the same way as a Fortune 500 CFO delegates much of the necessary ongoing work to his controllers.

Tax intelligence means gaining enough knowledge to direct those who serve you as well as the humility to defer to the experts when appropriate as well as to seek them out before the problems arise. Proactivity is key to tax management. The CFO (you) must plan ahead in all tax related areas–tax minimization, deduction maximization, large scale tax planning, estate planning and so on. To do this properly, expert support is a must.

Assemble your Intelligence Team.

*"Talent wins games but teamwork and
intelligence wins championships."*
~ Michael Jordan

Once you understand your Avatar and the Avatars of those in your inner circle as set forth in STAGES 1 and 2, perhaps the most important stage of all is STAGE 5 where you assemble the necessary personnel to create a complete Intelligence Team. At a minimum you need:

- An investment advisor.
- A tax advisor (who must liaise with the investment advisor).
- A financial counselor focused on retirement and estate planning.

All of these must work together. You cannot properly manage investments without considering the taxation aspects. You cannot plan a retirement without considering your current investment strategy. Unless you want to give much of your assets to the government once you pass, an estate plan is essential. And so on. The point is that a versatile Intelligence Team is essential to every aspect of your financial life, including planning, decision making, execution, and ongoing measurement. There is no way to successfully manage a complete financial plan without the support of expert team members.

Manage the Ecosystem. Become a 3%er.

"Your time is limited, so don't waste it living someone else's life.
Don't be trapped by dogma... Don't let the noise of other's
opinions drown out your own inner voice...
Have the courage to follow your heart and intuition.
They somehow already know what you truly want."
~ Steve Jobs

Now that your ecosystem has been built, what remains is the task of managing and maintaining it. This and only this, will take you into the financial world of those who earn and grow their wealth to becoming part of the wealthiest 3% of the population. Supported by your team, stay focused and progress toward your goals with unwavering determination. There is no mountain too tall, no sea too wide.

All is possible for those who take the proven steps to transform your Average Avatar into a Wealthy Avatar.

Summary

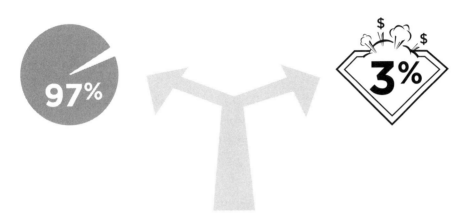

THE ROAD LESS TRAVELLED...

"The world is full of people who have dreams of playing at Carnegie Hall, of running a marathon, and of owning their own business. The difference between the people who make it across the finish line and everyone else is one simple thing: an action plan."
~ John Tesh

Let's face the harsh reality.
Most people will never become Three Percenters. They just won't.
It takes time. It requires commitment. It demands perseverance.
It's flat out hard on two entirely different levels.

First, discovering your Avatar is both challenging and highly emotional. What if you get it wrong? What if you "sort of" think you know it and in fact miss the mark? Consider the ramifications. You begin to filter your decisions through a flawed lens. You can't quite understand why things don't "feel right." You act at cross purposes to your highest self without being aware of why or how.

A plane that leaves California for Hawaii need only be off target by a single degree to miss the island completely, run out of fuel and fall like a rock into a vastly deserted ocean.

A lack of clarity or a blurred vision can keep you off course for years and life is far too short to take that risk.

Second, assembling an effective support team is equally difficult. No single individual can master the three pillars of financial, emotional and tax intelligence. By definition you need multiple specialists.

Not only that, on your own, you do not likely have the expertise to determine who are the most trusted, reputable and diligent experts to steward you and your plan to become a Three Percenter. Effective coordination of this cohesive team is a vital area where most fail because generally most specialists work for different firms and collaboration is not realistic.

High performance comes at a premium. Only an elite group can provide you with the complete package.

These two key points drive home a single, inevitable conclusion. You can't make the journey to becoming a Three Percenter on your own. Get help. Seek out trusted advisors and assemble your support team. Put yourself in a position to win by pulling together proven winners that reinforce your strength and compensate for any shortcomings.

Your future and the future of your family depend on you.

To protect them, you, in turn, must make the effort to find a team you can rely on--one that knows what it means to be a Wealthy Avatar.

CALL TO ACTION

"Wealth is the ability to fully experience life."
~ Henry David Thoreau

Action favors the bold.
Action drives results.
Action takes you from inertia into motion.
Results only come when you take action.

We invite you to contact us for a complimentary consultation. This consultation will allow you to see our proven process to becoming a Wealthy Avatar, so you can live in the ecosystem of the top 3% and break away from the herd. We will review your current situation, address any and all of your concerns, offer you counsel that is aligned with your goals and discuss what the odyssey to becoming a Three Percenter entails. You will find the process eye opening, enlightening and well worth your time.

Let us help you map out your journey to becoming a Wealthy Avatar.

To set an appointment, email us at:
WealthyAvatar@PeachCap.com
Or call us at (800) 624-0112.

We look forward to serving you.

THE AUTHORS

Ridgely Goldsborough, Esq., believes in taking complex and challenging topics, breaking them down to make sense out of them and sharing solutions that work. His Avatar is the "Problem Solver." To that end, he has written 15 books, created numerous audio programs, hosted his own television show (titled "Modest To Millions) and appeared on every major network (ABC, CBS, NBC, Fox and more) in an effort to share with others that success and wealth follow proven paths. He speaks around the world on the CEO circuit exposing elite financial minds to concepts with proven track records that can be adopted by anyone willing to commit to the process of wealth accumulation. He feels a particular desire to educate youth about proper money management and the eradication of senseless financial suffering that comes from poor choices.

Ridgely Goldsborough, J.D. attended the University of Virginia as an undergraduate and Whittier College School of Law as a graduate student. In addition he holds a Master Writing Certificate from UCLA and numerous other designations regarding online marketing. Ridgely lives in Pensacola with his lovely wife, Kathy, where they share a passion for fine dining, Southern hospitality and philanthropy.

David Miller CFP® believes in making the largest impact wherever he can through supporting organizations that further the betterment of society. His Avatar is the "Giver". David is a progressive thought leader in the financial services industry where he has been an integral connector in helping the industry bridge the problematic disconnect with millennials and older generations. At the age of 20 while attending University of Tennessee, David was on a team that managed a Large Cap Value portfolio for Tennessee Valley

Authority where they were instrumental in recommending the acquisition of Knoxville based CMH by famed investor Warren Buffett. He is the Founder and CEO of Peachtree Capital, a conglomerate of financial and accounting companies including a broker-dealer, RIA, CPA Firm, and Asset Management company.

David holds his Series 27, 24, 7, and 66 among other licenses. He received his BBA in Finance from Glocker Business School at UT in 2002 and his CFP® from Oglethorpe in 2008 in Atlanta. He is an avid community organizer, board member of the global CEO group, the Entrepreneurs Organization, involved with GCAPP, CHOA, Angel Investor with Atlanta Technology Angels, The Westside Future Fund for the revitalization of West Atlanta, Team Britton, Supporter of Colon Cancer Alliance, and former chairperson of various other non-profits. David and his loving wife, Suzanne, have 3 boys (Hudson, Deacon, & Paxton) and two dogs (schnauzer and labradoodle) and reside in Atlanta.